Contents

1
Introduction

Social geography is the study of issues concerning the human and social well-being of individuals on Planet Earth. More simply it may be expressed as a study of the factors contributing towards the quality of life of individuals. What is obvious from the study of geography and media reports from around the world is that, within the highly dependent and interrelated nature of the 'global village' in which we live today, the quality of life or well-being of the population varies considerably between continents, countries, regions and individuals. As one geographer put it 'the planetary framework. . . . works well for some and badly for many'.

One of the most recognisable differences in social and human well-being is seen when comparing the rich and poor countries of the world. Various terms are used to divide the world in such a way – developed/developing, rich/poor, advanced world/**third world** and, more recently with the publication of the Brandt Report, the **north/south**.

While such divisions can be useful in the study of geography, they have led to the formation of negative stereotyping within the minds of many people. The world is seen as being divided into two types of country, with third world countries of the 'south' characterised by undesirable features such as lack of development, simple, traditional technology, small-scale, subsistence production and poverty within a generally rural framework. On the other hand, the countries of the 'north' are seen within this simple division to be more 'developed' with desirable features such as modernised industry, advanced science and technology with larger scale production and wealth within a generally urban framework. The accuracy of such perceptions is highly questionable, as this book explores, although there can be no doubt that some features more common to third world countries such as relatively greater poverty, hunger and poorer medical provision are certainly aspects of life undesirable on Earth today. At the same time, there are fea-

THIS IS WHAT THEY CALL A NO-WIN SITUATION!

1.1

tures more commonly associated with the developed world which are equally undesirable for individuals and society as a whole such as urban crime, congestion, inner city decay and lack of open space. Fig. 1.1 reminds us that in spite of any differences that might exist between countries of the 'north' and 'south' in the world, both are equally important for the future of Mankind and that there is a real need for close cooperation between and a real understanding of each other in our world of limitless wants and finite resources.

Where is the third world?

The term 'third world' came into use in the post-war period with the grouping of the world's countries into various international blocs. The 'first world' was seen as the capitalist countries while the 'second world' was considered to be the socialist countries. The 'third world' was originally considered to be the countries of the non-aligned world but, over the years, they have more generally been characterised as the poor, non-industrialized, ex-colonial, dependent countries. Fig. 1.2 gives an indication of the general division of the world into the third world and the developed world.

Aspects of Social Geography: Change and Development

John Geddes

Assistant Head Teacher
Greenwood Academy, Irvine, Ayrshire

Kenneth Muir

Head of Geography
Greenwood Academy, Irvine, Ayrshire

Edward Arnold

First published 1987
by Edward Arnold (Publishers) Ltd
41 Bedford Square
London WC1B 3DQ

Edward Arnold (Australia) Pty Ltd
80 Waverley Road, Caulfield East
Victoria 3145, Australia

British Library Cataloguing in Publication Data
Geddes, John
    Aspects of social geography: change and
development.
    1. Economic development 2. Geography, Economic
I. Title   II. Muir, Kenneth
330.9   HD82

ISBN 0-7131-7614-8

Text set in 10/11pt Times
by Colset Private Limited, Singapore
Printed by Butler and Tanner Ltd, Frome, Somerset
Bound by W.H. Ware & Sons Ltd., Clevedon, Avon

Acknowledgements
The Publishers wish to thank the following for their
permission to use copyright photographs and material:

Christian Aid/Vicky White, cover & p6
United Nations pp12 top (John Isaac), 27 (P Almasy),
    71 bottom (WHO), 84 (John Isaac)
FAO/Government of Punjab p29
Foto Features p12 bottom
UNHCR/Julie Jessen-Petersen p24
WHO pp43 (World Bank/Y Hadar), 44 (D Deriaz),
    47 (Helen Keller Internat/N Cohen), 90 (I Guest)
J Allan Cash Ltd p53
Oxfam/Hannes Wallrafen p58
Steve Richards p71 top
Alex da Costa/J. Edward Milner p93.

Special thanks are due to Mary Muir and Helen Geddes
for help with collation of materials and proof reading
and to the pupils and staff of the geography department,
Greenwood Academy, Irvine.

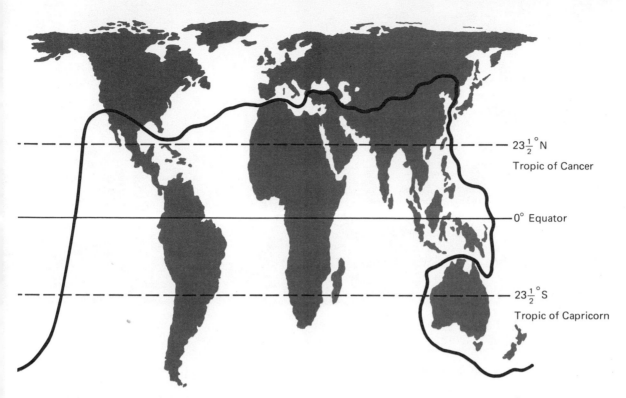

1.2 The developed 'North' and third world 'South' as seen by the Brandt Report. The Peters map projection shows the world's countries and continents in proportion to their relative sizes. This non-Eurocentric projection made a dramatic difference to the portrayal of the third world.

What is a third world country?

Indicators of development

Third world countries are usually considered to be poor and non-industrialised and are classed as such on the basis of some indicator(s) of economics such as those shown in Fig. 1.3. While such average indicators allow us to draw dividing lines between the rich and poor countries they should be regarded with some caution. Firstly, some third world countries can have indices that should place them among the more developed countries, e.g. Sri Lanka's % population literate (86%) exceeds that of Europe's Greece (84%). Also, the % literacy rate in Guyana (92%) is on a par with that found in European countries such as Italy and Bulgaria and yet is considerably higher than that of neighbouring Brazil (76%) and Venezuela (76%). Equatorial Guinea, considered by a recent *Economist* survey to be

	Income/head (U.S. $)	Energy consumed (kg coal equivalent)	Car ownership (cars/ 1000 pop.)	T.V. ownership (sets/ 1000 pop.)	Newspaper circulation (per 1000 pop.)	Telephones (per 1000 pop.)	Per capita G.N.P. (U.S. $)
U.K.	7548	4641	280	327	450	495	9050
JAPAN	7663	3575	215	537	569	479	10100
BRAZIL	2100	757	77	125	44	62	1890
NIGERIA	740	220	2.7	5.7	11	2.5	760
INDIA	217	199	1.5	1.7	20	4.1	260
U.S.A.	11695	10204	534	624	282	788	14090
BANGLADESH	113	46	0.4	0.9	<5	1.2	130
W. GERMANY	9341	5614	390	337	423	488	11420
U.S.S.R.	3400	5738	35	279	396	89	6350

1.3 Economic indicators of development

1.4 Modern flats and makeshift hovels in Bombay, India

among the ten bottom countries of the world in terms of standard of living has fewer people per hospital bed than the U.K., U.S.A., Canada, New Zealand and Ireland. Secondly, there are both developed and relatively less developed regions within many countries. In Brazil, for example, the state of Sao Paulo is economically very advanced while the states of the north-east and the Amazon are extremely poor. Even within the city of Sao Paulo, a simple contrast can be made between areas af extreme wealth and extreme poverty. The same pattern can also be seen in developed cities with affluent areas of suburbia contrasting sharply with some of the destitute areas of the inner city. Such contrasts of relative development and lack of development within one area are shown in Fig. 1.4.

A further criticism levelled at using **economic indicators** to define development and the third world countries is that they tend to define human well-being in terms of cash and a market economy with little indication of the living conditions of individuals and absolute levels of poverty and well-being. An alternative to using national income indicators is to consider **social indicators** such as hospital beds/1000 population and enrolment in primary schools. Such figures do give a clearer indication of the general level of human and social well-being but they do present a problem in that they tend to measure only the input or provision of service. They do not give an indication of how effective those inputs are at meeting basic human needs. More useful, therefore, are social indicators which measure the results of service provision and it is generally considered that life expectancy, infant mortality and adult literacy rates are among the most valuable indicators of human well-being. These three indices can be combined to produce a measure called the **Physical Quality of Life Index** (P.Q.L.I.) (Fig. 1.5). Dividing the world into developed and developing countries on this basis produces some which have a lower P.Q.L.I. than might be expected from their **Gross National Product** (G.N.P.) These include oil-rich countries such as Brunei, Saudi Arabia and the United Arab Emirites (U.A.E.). Also, others such as Sri Lanka and Jamaica have a higher P.Q.L.I. than their G.N.P. suggests. The table also shows, however, that no matter the indicator chosen, there are a group of countries that make up the very poorest both in terms of economics and social and human well-being and another group where indicators suggest a high standard of living and well-being.

The 1970s and 1980s have seen enormous changes within the developed and developing countries in areas which greatly affect human and social well-being – population movement and characteristics, medicine, health care, urbanization and farming. This book studies these and other topics affecting quality of life on Earth with special attention being paid to the changes and developments that have taken place and need to take place to improve the quality of life for all Mankind living in our 'global village'.

	Life expectancy at age one	Infant mortality rate (per 1000 live births)	Adult literacy rate (%)	P.Q.L.I. (index ranging from 0 to 100)	G.N.P. per capita (U.S. $)
BANGLADESH	56	133	26	41	130
AFGHANISTAN	54	205	20	20	230
INDIA	59	118	36	48	260
DEMOCRATIC KAMPUCHEA	43	160	48	36	70
ETHIOPIA	43	142	4	29	140
SRI LANKA	69	35	86	87	330
CHINA	68	38	66	80	290
KENYA	60	82	47	61	340
EGYPT	62	80	38	60	700
CAMEROON	56	117	40	49	800
NIGERIA	50	105	34	49	760
PHILIPPINES	66	50	83	81	760
PERU	63	99	72	64	1040
TUNISIA	64	85	38	54	1290
JAMAICA	72	28	96	92	1300
S. KOREA	65	29	88	88	2010
BRAZIL	69	71	76	74	1890
YUGOSLAVIA	72	32	87	89	2570
VENEZUELA	69	39	76	83	4100
HONG KONG	77	10	77	93	6000
U.K.	74	10	99	98	9050
JAPAN	77	6	99	100	10100
U.S.A.	75	10	99	98	14090
SAUDI ARABIA	56	103	25	49	12180
SWEDEN	77	7	100	100	12400
KUWAIT	73	23	60	84	18180
BRUNEI	71	15	64	87	21140
U.A.E.	71	45	54	76	21340

1.5 Physical quality of life index and G.N.P. per capita — 1985

1. Explain the links between the developed and the developing countries suggested in Fig. 1.1.

2. Which of the countries of the 'south' in Fig. 1.2 might be more appropriately grouped with the richer countries of the 'north'?

3. Use the economic indicators of development in Fig. 1.3 to group the countries into 'developed' and 'developing'. Select any anomolies to this general pattern and try to explain them.

4. With specific reference to examples taken from Fig. 1.5, describe and explain the general relationship between G.N.P. and P.Q.L.I.

5. Point to and explain any anomalies to the general pattern described in your answer to question 4.

2
Population, change and development

One in ten of all the people who have lived since the dawn of civilisation, some 5000 years ago, are alive today. Never before have there been so many people living on Planet Earth – and the world population today is probably the smallest it will ever be again. 30% of our planet is land, of which two fifths is desert or ice. The earth is the same size today as it was when first inhabited by people. It is now home to 4925 million people (1986 estimate) and growing by some 80 million per year. What are the implications of this?

To study 'Population, Change and Development', it is necessary to rely heavily on the use of statistics. The student should be aware that statistics can often mislead. They may be based on incomplete or biased surveys, or indeed be no more than inspired guesswork. The quality and reliability does vary from country to country. In Britain some 5700 people are employed by the Government, at a cost of £130 million a year, to collect and report the vast mass of official statistics.

The population census

United Nations definition: 'a **census** of population is the total process of collecting, compiling, evaluating, analysing and publishing demographic, economic and social data, pertaining, at a specific time, to all persons in a country.' An accurate count of population is important because every aspect of social administration, planning, research and political representation for an area is related to the number of people present. Data on age, family structure, housing and employment is central to governmental decision making with regard to the allocation of finance to a national health service, education, housing, environmental planning, and roads. The Rate Support Grant from the British Government is allocated on the basis of population in each area.

The census of population is central to this. In Britain, the first census was organised in 1801 and there has been a regular 10 yearly population count since then, (with the exception of 1941) the last one being in 1981. The country is divided into small areas (called enumeration districts) and every household receives a form to be completed. The British Census is compulsory, with legal sanctions to ensure that the information is complete and accurate. Fines can be imposed on any individual who fails to complete a census form. Governments have felt obliged to limit the number of questions, and avoid intrusive and sensitive areas in order to reduce fears of Government 'invasion of personal liberty'.

Because of the scale, complexity and expense, a full census has not yet been attempted more frequently than every 10 years. The time taken to process and publish the full results is considerable, from 1 year to 7 years. Such is the tempo of social change that the time lapse between censuses makes social trends impossible to predict. Britain attempted a 10% sample census in 1966, but cancelled a similar survey in 1976 due to cost. More and more countries, world wide, are now conducting their own census, often with financial backing and expertise from the United Nations. However in some developed countries, such as Norway and Sweden, the census has been abandoned altogether, and been replaced by very accurate and effective population registers. Sir John Boreham, recent head of the British Central Statistics Office, believes that the 1991 British Census may well be the last. The 1981 Census in Britain, was conducted at midnight on Sunday, 5th April, a time when most people were at home. 20 million householders had been issued with census forms. In areas with a large population of non-English speaking immigrants, interpreters were available. The cost worked out at just over £1 per person, not a large sum when considering the value of all the economic and social decisions taken as a result of the Census.

In Britain, additional data is collected on a number of occasions. All births, marriages and deaths have to be registered, and regular Government sponsored surveys report on the changing trends within British Society e.g. the General Household Survey, Population Trends and Social Trends.

Census data in developing countries

As mentioned earlier, most countries in the world now conduct a population census. However, there are problems collecting accurate census information in developing countries. Problems may include:

(a) nomadic groups which cross international frontiers e.g. Bedouin Nomads;

(b) remote villages in areas with limited accessibility, e.g. Burma;

(c) sheer size of the country in terms of both area (China) and numbers of villages/people (India);

(d) high population movement, e.g. Shanty towns in Sao Paulo;

(e) since a certain level of literacy is required, form filling is likely to be incomplete and inaccurate, e.g. only 21% of the adult population in Gambia is literate;

(f) suspicion of the motives behind a census, e.g. in China the population in a village may be linked to the taxes to be collected, and under-registration is not uncommon;

(g) the cost involved to a developing country, e.g. Bangladesh, cannot afford the high expenditure;

(h) lack of firm government control or civil war may mean areas not covered, e.g. Afghanistan, Iran.

As in the developed world, the developing countries have to make full use of their limited resources. Such is the rate of change in population numbers, structure and mobility, that the need for accurate data is of vital importance. It may take many years to prepare for change, e.g. a 'baby boom' will require increased expenditure on maternity provision and primary schooling.

1. Outline the methods used to collect accurate data for the ten-yearly national population census of the U.K. How is this data up-dated between censuses?

2. Discuss the problems of collecting accurate census information in developing countries. What are the possible social consequences for developing countries of planning with inadequate data?

3. Explain why the provision of social services may not meet the eventual level of demand even when accurate population data is available.

Demographic trends in the United Kingdom

Demography is the branch of science which deals with the statistics of births, deaths and population change. A population of people is continually changing as the individuals which make it up go through a life cycle from birth to death, and move around within and between countries at different times and for varying periods. For the U.K. population these changes can be quite considerable. During the year 1984, there were 702 000 births and 630 000 deaths; that is rather more than one birth and death every minute, which amounts to 2.1 million new individuals every three years.

As Fig. 2.1 reveals, the total population of the U.K. is growing slowly. However within the country there are obvious variations. In the period 1961 to 1986, the population change in England was up by 7.8%, whilst in Scotland there was a loss, of approximately 1.9%. Population projections, such as the one for the year 2001 are based on certain

	1961	1971	1986	2001	% change 1961–1986	% change 1961–2001
ENGLAND	43.6	46.0	47.0	48.2	+ 7.8	+10.6
WALES	2.6	2.7	2.8	2.8	+ 7.7	+ 7.7
SCOTLAND	5.2	5.2	5.1	5.0	− 1.9	− 3.8
NORTHERN IRELAND	1.4	1.5	1.6	1.7	+14.3	+21.0
TOTAL	52.8	55.5	56.5	57.7	+ 7.0	+ 9.3

2.1 Population of U.K. (millions) – 1961, 1971, 1986 and projected 2001

	Age 0–4		5–14	15–29	30–44	45–59	60–64	65–74	75 +	Total
1951	4.3		7.1	10.2	11.2	9.6	2.5	3.7	1.8	50.3
1986	3.6		7.1	13.4	11.4	9.2	3.1	5.0	3.7	56.5
2001*	3.9		7.9	10.6	13.0	10.9	2.7	4.7	3.1	57.7

	Age	0–14	15–59	60 +	65 +
1951		22%	62%	16%	11%
1986		19%	60%	21%	15%
2001		20%	61%	19%	15.2%
					1901 figure
					5%

2.2 Age and population structure of U.K. (millions above; percentage below) – 1951, 1986, and projected 2001

assumptions, regarding the number of births, deaths and migrants. Such estimates are frequently wrong, yet are useful nevertheless, as they may indicate a trend.

Population statistics also reveal the structure of that population. In Fig. 2.2, the number of people found in various age groupings has been calculated for 1951, 1986 and estimated for 2001. Between 1951 and 1986 there has been a decline in the numbers of young children, a substantial rise in the number of young adults and a 47% increase in those aged 60 and over. Such a change in population structure has implications when the government allocates funds for health and the social services. Fig. 2.3 lists selected social and economic needs of population groups by age. Again, within the country there are significant geographical variations. Fig. 2.4 illustrates the differences in structure within Britain and the Scottish Regions, and between the various ethnic groups. Between 1971 and the 1981 Census, there were about 6 million births and slightly fewer deaths in the U.K. Although the net effect on the total population is not great, the total effect on the structure of the population is enormous. This is also true for the changes resulting from migration.

Fig. 2.5, is a dynamic model of population change. Population changes as a direct result of a number of competing factors. The impact of migration will be dealt with in Chapter 6.

4. Study Figs. 2.1 and 2.2. In your own words outline the main demographic trends in the period 1986 to 2001.

5. Study Fig. 2.4. Identify any differences within Scotland in terms of population structure. When comparing the Scottish structure with that of the various ethnic groups, what basic differences can be noted? Consult Fig. 2.3, and describe the implications in terms of social and economic needs.

6. Look at Fig. 2.5. Say why the model gives a more dynamic picture of population than a precise figure obtained from a census return?

		Population index		
Age Group	Social and economic needs	1971	1984	2001
LESS THAN 1	Maternity, health visiting, preventative medicine	126	100	107
1–4	Daycare nursery education	127	100	110
5–15	Compulsory education	117	100	105
16–19	Further and higher education, employment	82	100	76
16–44 (female)	Maternity provision	88	100	96
20–59	Employment, housing, transport	93	100	102
60–74	Retirement pensions	99	100	93
OVER 75	Pension, health care, sheltered housing	75	100	116

2.3 Selected social and economic needs of population groups by age (population index for 1984 = 100)

	% 0–15	% 16–44	% 45–60/65*	% Pensionable age +	% born in U.K.
GREAT BRITAIN	22.3	40.4	19.7	17.7	93.7
SCOTLAND	23.2	40.5	19.5	16.8	97.2
BORDERS	21.5	37.2	19.8	21.5	97.6
GRAMPIAN	22.8	41.4	18.9	16.9	96.8
CENTRAL	23.9	41.2	19.4	15.6	97.6
HIGHLAND	24.5	40.1	18.8	16.6	97.4
STRATHCLYDE	23.7	40.6	19.6	16.1	97.4
WESTERN ISLES	25.1	35.1	18.4	21.5	98.5
WEST INDIAN	25.0	53.0	22.0		49.0
INDIAN	33.0	50.0	17.0		33.0
PAKISTAN	45.0	42.0	13.0		39.0
BANGLADESH	54.0	34.0	12.0		32.0
CHINESE	30.0	58.0	13.0		20.0

2.4 Population structure within Britain, within Scotland and within ethnic groups in Britain – 1985

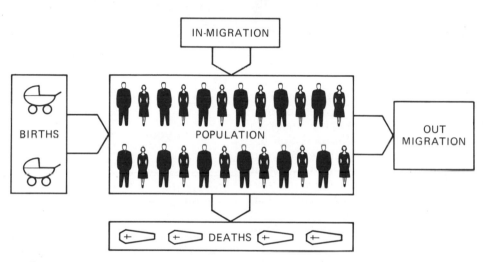

2.5 Dynamic model of population change

Fertility measures

The **fertility** of a population is an indicator of the tendency for it to increase by births, and is important in explaining and projecting population change. The most basic measure of fertility is the **crude birth rate**, which can be formally stated as the number of live births, in a year, per 1000 of the population. The problem with this indicator is that it is based on the total population of a country, and not that proportion of the population most affected; that is women of child bearing age.

The **general fertility rate** takes the number of women aged 15 to 44 as the denominator, and can be defined as the number of live births in a year, per 1000 women aged 15 to 44. Even more sophisticated measures involve **age specific rates**, when narrower age bands are used, e.g. women aged 25 to 29. There are many influences on birth rates (some of which will be reviewed in more detail later) such as age of marriage, divorce rates (over 90% of births still occur within marriage), availability of contraception and family planning provision, abortion policy, surgical sterilization, religion, government policy and socially accepted family size, level of economic development and status of women in society.

Death measures

In Britain, the two main measures causing a loss of population are emigration and death. Again the basic statistical measure is the **crude death rate**, indicating death regardless of the structure of the

2.6 Drought ravages Africa. A mother and severely malnourished children in Ethiopia

SUMMARY

Crude Birth Rate	$=$ $\dfrac{\text{Total births in a year}}{\text{Total population}}$	$\times \dfrac{1000}{1}$
General Fertility Rate	$=$ $\dfrac{\text{Total births in a year}}{\text{Total women aged 15 to 44}}$	$\times \dfrac{1000}{1}$
Age Specific Birth Rate	$=$ $\dfrac{\text{Total Births to women in specific age bands}}{\text{Number of women in same age bands}}$	$\times \dfrac{1000}{1}$
Crude Death Rate	$=$ $\dfrac{\text{Total deaths in a year}}{\text{Total Population}}$	$\times \dfrac{1000}{1}$
Age Specific Death Rate	$=$ $\dfrac{\text{Deaths in specific age band}}{\text{Number in same age band}}$	$\times \dfrac{1000}{1}$
Infant Mortality Rate	$=$ $\dfrac{\text{Number of deaths under 1 year}}{\text{Number of live births in year}}$	$\times \dfrac{1000}{1}$
Growth Rate or Natural Increase	$=$ Crude Birth Rate – Crude Death Rate	

population. For example, Sweden has an ageing population with over 16% of the population over 65. The crude death rate is 11 per 1000. In Singapore, only 5% of the population is over 65, and the crude death rate is 6 per 1000. Does this mean that Sweden's death rate is almost twice that of Singapore? Does it imply that health care provision in Sweden is inferior? No, in fact, since Singapore's population is very youthful, one would not expect as many deaths as in an elderly population.

Age specific death rates can give a clearer comparison between two countries. (See Summary table below.) A third indicator of death is the **infant mortality rate**, calculated by the number of infant deaths per 1000 live births in a year. Crude death rates and infant mortality rates are also influenced by a number of factors, principally: incidence and prevalence of epidemic and endemic diseases (see Chapter 4), stage of economic development, health care provision and the age structure of the population. The overall **growth rate** of a population is an indicator of the rate of population increase, and is calculated by substracting the death rate from the birth rate. From the growth rate it is possible to calculate the **doubling time**, in years, of a country's population. For example a growth rate in population of 3% per year results in the population of that country doubling in 30 years, assuming no change in birth and death rates nor any migration. Fig. 2.8, shows the marked variations in population statistics in different parts of the world.

2.7 Crowded city street in Jaipur, India

7. Measurement of population presents a number of problems to demographers. The list below contains a number of ratios used in population studies. Choose three of these and for each give a detailed account of the manner in which the ratio is obtained and the reasons for using it: Crude Birth Rate; General Fertility Rate; Infant Mortality Rate; Rate of Natural Increase.

World population

The period 1950 to 1985 has witnessed a massive growth in world population. In 1900, global numbers stood at 1500 million; by 1950 a further 1000 million had been added. By 1975 the 4000 million mark was passed and by 1985 the total was estimated to be 4845 million. This rapid growth was described by geographers in the 1970s as the 'population explosion'. Growth today still exceeds one million extra people on this planet every 5 days. The rate of natural increase is now around 1.7% per year, which if continued would result in a doubling of the world's population in 41 years. However, the trend is downwards, and the future is more optimistic than ten years ago when the growth rate was 2% per year, and the doubling time was 35 years. Fig. 2.8 reveals quite marked differences in world birth, death and growth rates. Various attempts have been made over the years to design models to describe, explain and predict population change. One of the earlier theories was proposed by the Rev. Thomas Malthus in 1798, when he stated that the population of a country, if unchecked by war or famine, would eventually outstrip the available food supply. On a world scale this has not happened, due to a number of factors not foreseen by Malthus: improvements in agricultural production; the opening up of new granaries in the Steppes, the Prairies, the Pampas and Australia; improvements in communications and transport such as refrigerated shipping; the movement towards a global economy with large-scale trading by all nations.

8. Study Fig. 2.8, which shows various population statistics for selected countries in the developed and the developing world. Make a list of the six countries with the highest birth rates. Make a list of those countries with the lowest birth rates. Comment on your results. Can you detect any apparent relationship betwen the rate of natural increase and infant mortality rates?

9. The newspaper article on page 14 argues that the shortage of food in our planet is political and not economic. Explain why the author suggests this is the case and comment on the meaning of the title.

Region or country	Mid 1985 population estimate (millions)	Crude birth rate (per 1000)	Crude death rate (per 000)	Growth rate/ natural increase %	Doubling time in years	Projected population in 2000 (millions)	Infant mortality rate (per 000)	% population under 15/ over 65	Life expectancy (years)	Urban population (%)
EGYPT	48.3	37	10	2.7	26	67.3	80	40/4	57	44
GAMBIA	0.8	49	29	2.0	35	1.0	193	43/3	35	21
NIGERIA	91.2	48	17	3.1	22	156.5	105	48/2	50	28
ETHIOPIA	36.0	43	22	2.1	33	54.8	142	45/3	43	15
SAUDI ARABIA	11.2	42	12	3.0	23	18.9	103	43/3	56	70
BANGLADESH	101.5	45	17	2.8	25	146.2	133	47/3	48	15
INDIA	762.2	34	13	2.2	32	990.6	118	39/3	53	23
INDONESIA	168.4	34	12	2.2	32	226.2	87	41/3	55	22
CHINA	1042.0	19	8	1.1	65	1197.0	38	34/5	65	21
JAPAN	120.8	13	6	0.6	110	128.1	6.2	22/10	77	76
U.S.A.	238.9	16	9	0.7	100	268.0	10.5	22/12	75	74
MEXICO	79.7	32	6	2.6	27	112.8	53	42/4	66	70
BRAZIL	138.4	31	8	2.3	30	187.1	71	37/4	63	68
BOLIVIA	6.2	42	16	2.7	26	9.5	124	44/3	51	46
SWEDEN	8.3	11	11	0.0	6930	7.9	7.0	19/16	76	83
UNITED KINGDOM	56.4	13	12	0.1	630	57.0	10.1	20/15	73	76
WEST GERMANY	61.0	10	11	−0.2	–	58.4	10.1	17/15	74	94
U.S.S.R.	278.0	20	10	1.0	71	316.0	32	25/10	69	64
AUSTRALIA	15.8	16	7	0.9	82	17.2	10.3	25/10	75	86
WORLD	4845	27	11	1.7	41	6135	81.0	35/6	62	41

2.8 Selected population statistics – 1985

Malthus no: malnutrition yes

The spectre of famine in the midst of plenty, of Africans starving while Europeans and Americans bewail their surpluses, haunts us inescapably.

Last year the EEC spent £65 million on taking fruit and vegetables off the market and destroying them to prevent a glut.

The world as a whole is far better able to feed itself than anyone would have thought possible a few years ago.

Look back through press cuttings and you will find that, in the mid-1970s, the doom-mongers were warning us that disaster threatened unless something was done about population control.

The United Nations set up a new agency, the International Fund for Agricultural Development. World food stocks were said to be at their lowest since the Second World War, a serious crop failure would send prices through the roof.

At about the same time, Professor Jan Tinbergen of the Netherlands, winner of a Nobel prize for economics, reported that drastic changes were needed to ward off "mass starvation".

Then the tune changed. A report prepared for the UN World Food Council in February last year admitted that many of the predictions made a decade earlier were wrong, including the assumption that rising demand would outpace cereal production. Nevertheless, chronic hunger remained a "problem" for millions of people.

How so? The bleak doctrine that the human race is multiplying so fast that sooner or later it will exhaust its natural resources is, if not wholly discredited, at least now open to doubt. For the time being, the world is well able to produce all the food it needs. People should not go hungry, but they do.

The October issue of the UN Food and Agriculture Organization outlook report shows how astonishingly predictions have changed in a short space of time. Far from food stocks being dangerously low, it is forecast that world cereal production will reach a record 1,884 million tonnes this year. Global carryover stocks are put at 358 million tonnes, more than last year's entire North American grain crop.

Band Aid's brilliantly successful campaign to assist famine relief in Ethiopia and the Sudan has so far raised £52 million.

"Ample supplies" of edible oils are forecast, with next year's output reaching some 68 million tonnes. Cold stores are groaning under the weight of unsold meat carcasses, and New Zealand farmers recently slaughtered thousands of sheep in protest at low prices.

How has all this happened? The weather has certainly helped. Except in the Sahel region of Africa, there have been few, if any, significant crop failures. Even in Africa, the drought is over in most areas, and several countries, including Kenya, Zimbabwe and Malawi, will have surpluses for export this year!

But the most important factor is the enormous advance in technology. New crop strains have been developed which give yields that, a generation ago, would have been inconceivable. Pesticides, for all the alleged damage they do to the environment, have dramatically reduced the ravages from pests and diseases.

Advances in veterinary medicine, which include the controversial use of hormone implants and antibiotics as growth promoters, have produced larger and healthier animals.

Yet, almost coincidentally with its optimistic supply forecasts, the FAO has also issued a dispiriting little booklet pointing out that hunger and malnutrition, far from being on the wane, are still increasing.

Every year 15 million children die of hunger-related causes, it says. Some 435 million people, more than one-fifth of the world's population, are undernourished. Of these, more than 300 million are in Asia and the Pacific, and 40 million in Latin America.

Drought, natural disasters, war, soil erosion and deforestation can be blamed in some cases, but the main culprits are lack of organization and the reluctance of governments to allot sufficient priority to agriculture or to give farmers the incentives to produce at more than subsistence level.

The message is blindingly obvious: our failure to ensure that everyone has enough to eat is political, not economic.

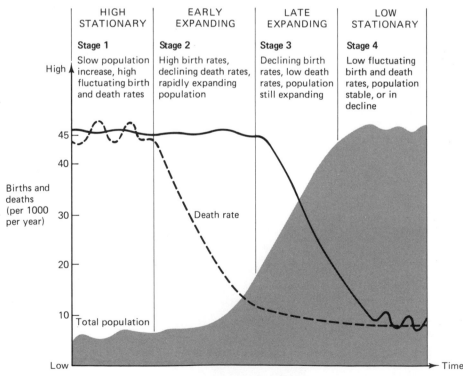

2.9 Demographic transition model

Based upon the trends in birth, death and growth rates, in both the developed and developing world, a more advanced theory has been formulated, the **Demographic Transition Model** (See Fig. 2.9). This suggests that growth rates can be divided up into four distinct stages. In stage 1, the birth and death rates are high and fluctuate according to the incidence of disease or famine. The total population is relatively stable over a long period. No country in the world today exhibits high birth and death rates as suggested in the model, although there probably exist within a number of countries, small groups of people at this stage of development. (For example in the more remote areas of Papua New Guinea or Brazil.)

Stage 2 reveals an expanding population based on declining death rates, although the birth rates remain high. Originally it was believed that the process of industrialization was the most important factor bringing about the movement from stage 1 to stage 2. It is now generally recognised that such a trend follows from improvements in public health and medical advances. Countries with a growth rate in excess of 2% are probably within stage 2.

Stage 3 reveals a decline in the birth rate, resulting in a fall in growth rates. The death rate continues to be low. Countries within stage 3 still show a growing population in the region of 1% to 2% per year.

Stage 4 completes the so called 'population cycle', and includes those areas with low, slightly fluctuating birth rates, low death rates and a stable population. Indeed in a few countries, a decline in population has been notable in recent years. (Hungary, West Germany and Denmark.)

Such a model of population is optimistic, suggesting that in time, those countries presently experiencing high growth rates i.e. stage 2 should progress through stage 3, and possibly even reach stage 4. The 'population explosion' of the 1970s is already showing signs of moderating, and it is to be hoped that world growth rates will continue to decline.

Case study: China . . . population change and policy

China with 22% of the world's population, has more people than any other country. (Mid 1985 estimate 1042 million.) During the 1950s, China's population was rapidly growing at over 2.2% per year, a figure which was later increased to over 2.6% during the peak years of population explosion, 1962 to 1973. In this period, China's population grew from 658 million to 892 million, an increase of some 35%.

This rapid growth can be attributed to a number of factors:

1. A drastic decline of the death rate, due to improved living conditions and medical and health care more widely available. Epidemic diseases were increasingly controlled or even eliminated. In 1949, the death rate was in excess of 25 per 1000, a figure which has now been reduced to 9 per 1000.

2. Life expectancy has increased from 45 years in 1949 to 65 years in 1985. This combined with the substantial drop in infant mortality rate has allowed many more children to survive the first few years of life and become adults. These adults now live longer, and have children themselves.

3. The birth rate was high and remained high during the years of maximum growth. Prior to 1971 there was no nationwide effort to encourage birth control. Indeed, there were a number of factors which encouraged and maintained a high birth rate. Firstly, the income of a peasant family was linked to the number of labourers it had. The state was unable to provide social insurance, and children (especially boys) increased family income and traditionally took care of their parents when they became old. To be sure of two surviving sons, the optimum number of births was seven per family. The vast majority of adults had no access to contraceptive methods. As a result, China's population changed from a high birth – high death rate – low growth rate pattern typical of old China, to the high birth – low death rate – high growth rate pattern in the first 20 years after the founding of the People's Republic. This can be linked to stages 1 and 2 of the demographic transition model.

Since 1973, and especially from 1979, family planning has assumed a very high government priority. China's industrial and agricultural progress was offset by the population 'explosion'. It has been estimated that some 200 million couples will marry and have children in the years 1985 to 2000. If each couple have two children, the total population would grow to at least 1300 million, with continued growth until the mid 2020s when the population would exceed 1800 million. The government decided to introduce, in 1979, a series of far reaching proposals to reduce the birth rate. The target is to keep the population within 1200 million, requiring a drop in the birth rate to about 16 per 1000, a decrease of nearly one fourth of the the present rate. The basic demands of family planning are late marriage, late childbirth and having fewer babies. Couples are now urged to have only one child. The slogan in 1979 was that births should be, 'late, spaced and few'. Couples who limited their reproduction to this level would enjoy many advantages, including priority in housing, access to private plots for cultivation, higher educational standards for the child, increased grain rations, better state care for elderly members of the family and cash subsidies. Such benefits are withheld from those couples who choose to have two or more children. At present some 20 million couples have signed a 'one child only' pledge.

Apart from the economic measures above, the policy is backed by publicity and education on the value of family planning and the advantages of a small family. Advice is freely and widely available, and should there be an unwanted pregnancy, induced abortion is available and surgical sterilization is encouraged among couples who have already had two or more children. Other factors which could reduce birth rates include migration to cities and towns, more employment opportunities for women, and a rise in general living standards.

This rigid one child family planning policy, has met with resistance in the more remote, and the most fertile areas, yet would appear to be well supported in industrial and urbanized areas. Farmers still see the advantages of extra 'labourers', and generally prefer sons. This is due to the custom of married daughters leaving home and 'belonging' to the husband's family. The Chinese press has highlighted a rise in female infanticide in rural areas. Presumably such parents have killed their daughter in favour of gaining another chance to produce a son.

The outcome of this policy is zero growth by the year 2000, which would produce dramatic changes in population structure and overthrow the traditional Chinese acceptance of the large extended family. If successful, within 50 years, over a quarter of China's population will be over 65 years, resulting in conflict and competition over limited public funds.

The Chinese experiment is a good example of positive action to combat a perceived problem. The social consequences are clear, with individual choices and beliefs being of secondary importance to state policy. By the year 2000, China should have reached stage 4 of the demographic transition model.

10. Study Fig. 2.9 and the case study on China. The model is based upon the stages of population growth typical of most West European countries, which have undergone Agricultural and Industrial Revolutions.
   a) Describe and account for stages 1, 2, 3 and 4.
   b) Today many developing countries tend to typify stage 2. With reference to any named area in the developing world, outline the social

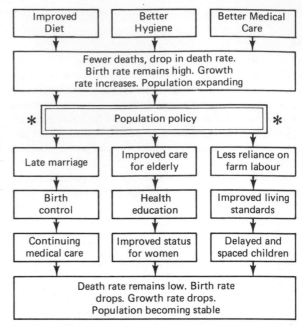

2.10 Model showing factors affecting birth and death rates

and economic problems arising from such a population pattern.
   c) Discuss difficulties confronting a developing country advancing from stage 2 to stage 3 of the model.
   d) What steps have the Chinese taken to move from stage 3 to stage 4?

Population and development

Perceptions of population issues have changed over the years. In the 1960s and 1970s, the general feeling was that the population explosion was bound to cause mass famines, widespread unrest and an overload on the world's environmental resources. The only hope, it was suggested, was a massive contraceptive campaign to reduce the fertility of the poor 'masses' in the developing world. Poverty was considered the fault of population growth. In the 1980s, the third world countries began to argue the case that population growth was more a result of poverty than a cause.

Desperately poor people often needed many children because they had no other form of security in illness or old age; no other kind of help in fields and homes; no comparable source of joy and pride and change in lives that were often stagnant with poverty. Given the importance of children to the poor, and given the fact that up to half of their children could be expected to die before the age of five, it was hardly surprising that the poor families of the developing countries had, on average, twice

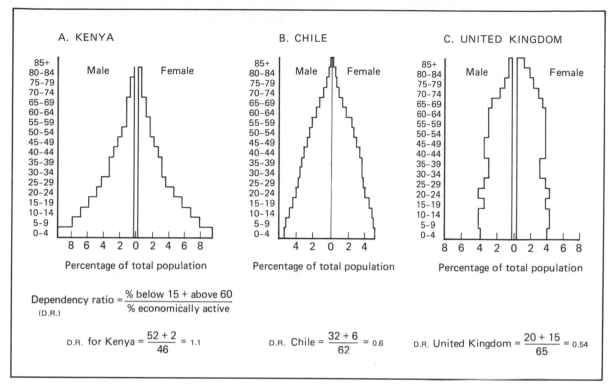

2.11 Population pyramids: Kenya; Chile; U.K.

as many children as the rich families in the industrialized world. Birth rates had fallen dramatically in the industrialized countries after living standards had begun to rise and long before the widespread availability of cheap and effective contraceptives. Therefore it would appear that the key to population stability in the developing world is through increased economic development, re-inforced by a clear policy on family planning.

It has been stated that, 'Political revolution can take place overnight, technological revolution takes a few years, but a social revolution can take a decade or more.'

The countries where birth rates have recently most declined have usually been those which have managed to spread the benefits of development. In Kerala, India, the hope of a better life, improved health care provision, the improved status and education of women, and adequate food supplies, has brought about a fall in birth rates. The Brandt Report of 1980 warns that the widespread trends of fertility decline may create the impression that the situation is under control. International support for population policies is flagging at precisely the time when the commitment to, and political acceptance of, family planning policies is spreading in the third world. (See Fig. 2.10, a model showing factors affecting birth and death rates.)

Population structure

Age-sex pyramids are constructed using either the percentage, or the number, of men and women in various age groupings of the population of a country. Population pyramids allow a visual comparison of the structure to be made between countries, as well as graphically showing changes in structure over a period of time. Demographers, with the aid of computers, can theoretically vary birth, death and migration rates and can visually show and predict future population structures.

Fig. 2.11 shows three contrasting population structures: those of Kenya, Chile and the United Kingdom. Pyramid A clearly reveals the structure of a developing country still firmly in stage 2 of the Demographic Transition Model. There are relatively few old people, and the pyramid has a very wide base, indicating a very high birth rate with limited control over infant mortality. The population is very youthful with 52% under 15 years of age. Life expectancy is low, but if the death rate drops, there will soon be an incredible number of children entering the economically active stage, and entering their reproductive years.

Pyramid B still tapers towards the top in a clearly structured pattern. The birth rate is still fairly high, with less infant mortality, a longer life expectancy, and a greater proportion of elderly people. Such a pyramid shows many of the features of a country passing through stage 3 of the Demographic Transition Model.

The 'bullet' shaped pyramid C is fairly typical of a country with a stable population. The numbers are more or less even up to the age of 60. The United Kingdom has a high proportion of elderly people, low birth and death rates and a very low infant mortality rate. In the U.K. women have a longer life expectancy than men. This was not always the case. Forty years ago the positions were reversed but now death during childbirth, once the most common cause of death in young women, is no longer a major killer.

Dependency ratio

The population of a country is frequently divided up into major groupings. The **non-economically active** or **dependent population** consists of those too young to work, normally considered to be below 15, and those who have reached retirement age, usually taken to be 60. Clearly such calculations are based on weak assumptions. In the U.K., a substantial number of youths continue with full-time education for many more years, and the retirement age for men is officially 65, although many women and men work beyond this. The term, **economically active** is used to describe that group of the population between 15 and 60. Using the formula below we can calculate the different dependency ratios for the three countries in Fig. 2.11.

$$\text{Dependency ratio} = \frac{\% \text{ non economically active}}{\% \text{ economically active}}$$

Implications of population structure

In developing countries such as Kenya, Ghana Bolivia or Papua New Guinea, a very youthful population implies that the limited financial resources available should, for a number of years, be concentrated on facilities for the young – maternity hospitals and primary schools. Since the dependency ratio is so high, e.g. 0.9 in Ghana, this means that for every worker there is almost one 'dependent' to be cared for. This puts a tremendous strain on a country. This youthfulness of a population, or juvenility, is one of the recognised indicators of development used to differentiate the developed and the developing world.

A youthful population means that there will be a sizeable group of young people entering the labour market in the next few years and employment will

be a major problem. As yet such countries do not need to invest substantial funds in the provision of 'pensions' or additional facilities for the elderly.

In a developed country such as the United Kingdom where the dependency ratio is low, there are almost two workers for every dependent. Such a situation eases the burden upon those workers, but there are nevertheless problems in finding jobs for all those workers. In the mid to late 1980s, unemployment was paradoxically the highest it had been in 50 years; at the same time more people had jobs than ever before in Britain's history. Social services in a developed country with a population structure similar to that of Britain have to balance the demands for resources at both ends of the pyramid.

11. a) Examine Fig. 2.12. Name the model which typifies the population structure of a developed country, and the one which typifies a less developed country.
    b) Describe and explain each of the two models.
    c) Neither of these population structures represents a permanent situation. Discuss how and under what circumstances the structure can change.
    d) With reference to specific countries or regions, discuss the reasons for and the problems associated with expanding populations; and contracting populations.

12. Draw population pyramids for the following structures, and outline the main distinguishing features. Give examples of actual countries, cities or areas for:
    i) a contracting population;
    ii) a stable population after recent major war losses;
    iii) an expanding population with large emigration of young males.

Population characteristics

In addition to population structure, juvenility and dependency ratios, there are a number of other characteristics that should be mentioned. Migration and the process of urbanization are dealt with in Chapters 6 and 5. In the remainder of this Chapter, attention will be focused on employment, literacy and education, life expectancy and infant mortality.

Employment, unemployment and underemployment

A major problem in the third world is not so much a lack of work, but more a lack of income. Protection against economic hardship is almost unknown in such countries. Millions of landless and near

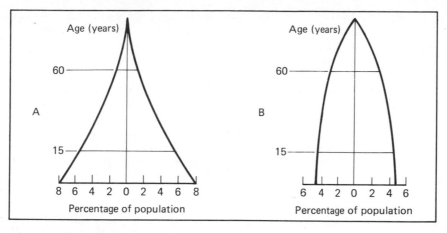

2.12 Models of population structure

landless peasants work long hours for meagre returns almost every day of the year. Unemployment benefits, trade unions, the right to strike, sick pay, pensions, holidays and even weekends are unknown to them. They must work simply to survive.

Geographers now recognise that the concept of 'unemployment' is unsuitable for describing the workforce of societies such as rural Java. The term 'underemployment', implying that peasants spend many hours in 'enforced idleness' is thought more appropriate. However even this description misses the point. Recent studies in Asia, especially in India and Indonesia, show that peasants, (whether or not they own land) work long hours throughout the year in a wide range of agricultural and off-farm jobs. The return for their labour, however, is pitifully small. They do not lack employment as such. What they lack is employment ensuring enough income to cover their basic needs.

According to the International Labour Organisation, (I.L.O.) the Asian labour force is

	% illiterate (over 15 years)			% adults (over 25) with no schooling	% of primary age pupils at school	Newspapers sold (per 000 people)
	Total	Men	Women			
ETHIOPIA	96	91	99.8	98	43	1
NIGERIA	66	54	77	88	98	9
BRAZIL	23	22	25 (Total)	32	93	44
	15	12	18 Urban			
	42	40	43 Rural			
BANGLADESH	74	62	86 (Total)	82	74	16
	51	42	66 Urban			
	76	65	88 Rural			
INDIA	65	52	80 (Total)	72		20
	40	27	54 Urban	46	70	
	72	60	87 Rural	78		
CHINA	34	20	48 Total	not known	100	33
	17	9	26 Urban			
	37	23	53 Rural			
U.S.A.	0.5	–	–	3	100	269
U.K.	0.5	–	–	2	100	421
U.S.S.R.	0.2	–	–	36	100	405

2.13 Education and literacy characteristics

19

likely to expand by 51% by the year 2000, the African by 75%, and the Latin American by 90%. Spectacular increases are projected for individual countries. Mexico and Peru could double their workforce in the next 20 years. Brazil's workforce could rise by 30 million in the same time. According to the I.L.O., 1000 million new jobs, most of them in the third world, will have to be created by the year 2000, in order to keep pace with demand. Such are the implications of changing population structure.

The chance of industry absorbing this vast army is effectively nil. Western technology has resulted in saving jobs in agriculture and destroyed scores of jobs in traditional village industries such as pottery, weaving and leatherwork. Such capital investment and imported technology offers little hope for the vast number of people looking for paid employment. There have been some successes, (such as in South Korea, Taiwan, Singapore and Hong Kong) but even so their range of products is limited, being mostly footwear, textiles and electrical goods.

Almost everyone in the third world works. But there is very little 'wage' employment. Most work, especially by women and children is for subsistence. The real problem is insufficient opportunity to earn an adequate income, either on family farms or in paid employment.

In Java, many men work for short periods in agriculture, then migrate for several months to the cities to find casual work, such as pedicab drivers or construction labourers. During the course of a single day, peasants may work in two or three 'jobs' as well as doing household chores. For example, a woman may work as a small trader at the village market for a couple of hours in the early morning, then harvest rice for wages on a neighbour's field, fetch fodder for the family's cattle during the afternoon, and weave mats for sale during the evening. A man might work on a road building site in the morning, then do some repairs on the family home, and during the evening go fishing or weed his fields. Many landless and small landowning households in Java earn up to 80% of their income in off-farm jobs.

Official statistics are based on a workforce aged 10 years and over, but children from 'working poor' households begin working from the age of five or six. Their contributions to the household are generally not in the form of direct wages. Rather their work frees parents from domestic tasks so they can take jobs outside the home. Children do chores around the house such as looking after younger brothers and sisters, sweeping the house and yard, and collecting firewood, fodder and water.

Education and literacy

An important battle in the search for development is the campaign against illiteracy. Over the last three decades poor countries, such as Burma and Peru, have greatly reduced the percentage of illiterates. According to the United Nations Educational, Scientific and Cultural Organisation,

A nation lost for words

Definitions of functional illiterates include people unable to fill out a form, read a medicine bottle or a newspaper, look up a telephone number or use a bus timetable.

They are mechanics who cannot read manuals, clerks who bungle menial jobs, shoppers who cannot select supermarket bargains, factory workers unable to tell 'High Voltage' from 'Fire Exit'. In America, they are one out of five adults (official government figures). Unofficially, they are one in three.

How at least 26 million people in the world's richest nation can emerge from school still unable to decipher the morning's headlines without a laborious effort is as mysterious as it is scandalous.

Cynics say illiteracy escapes the full blast of Congressional scrutiny because its victims are at the bottom of the social, economic and voter-power strata. Only five per cent of illiterates are reached by literacy programmes and government funding equals just over £1 a year for every illiterate adult.

The government accepts the following functional illiteracy figures produced by the University of Texas: Adult men – 17 per cent; adult women – 23 per cent; white adults – 16 per cent; black adults – 44 per cent and Hispanics – 56 per cent.

It is estimated officially that 2.3 million people a year become functionally illiterate adults, far outweighing the number who complete adult literacy courses successfully. If this is true, at least 60 million American adults would be incapable of reading this article.

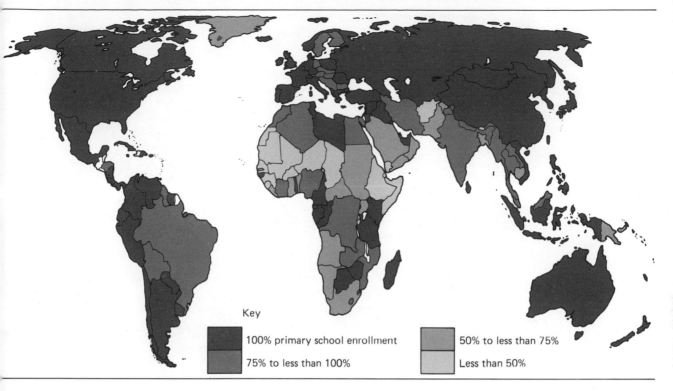

Key

■ 100% primary school enrollment ▨ 50% to less than 75%

■ 75% to less than 100% □ Less than 50%

2.14 Primary school enrolment – 1983

(UNESCO) in 1985 the developing world had an **illiteracy** rate of 29%. It is hoped that this could fall to 26% by 1995. Nevertheless, the 850 million illiterates in 1985 could increase to over 950 million by the year 2000. The burden of illiteracy falls hardest on the poorest and most disadvantaged groups, landless rural peasants, women and slum dwellers.

Fig. 2.13 clearly shows the variation in literacy rates in selected countries. Note the differences in, a) men and women, and b) urban and rural areas. Two further indicators of education and literacy levels are shown on this figure.

Mass public education is a recent phenomenon. Until the Industrial Revolution in the U.K. most schooling was run by the church, and publicly financed education only expanded rapidly towards the end of the nineteenth century. Within the U.K., children are legally required to attend school between the ages of 5 and 16, and over 22% remain in full-time education beyond that point. Many other developed countries, such as Japan or the U.S.A., have well over 50% of their 18 year olds still in full-time study.

In the developing world, 4 out of every 10 people are of school age. In India, 70% of children will enrol in primary school, and approximately half will reach the fourth grade. Only 10% will go on to a secondary school. Indeed, according to UNESCO, over 72% of the over 25's have had no schooling at any time.

Fig. 2.14 reveals the contrasts in primary school enrolment throughout the world.

Education and literacy are regarded as crucial for development. However, over half of all money spent on education in the developing world is used to fund secondary and higher education. In many cases this education is modelled on European lines. Valuable as this may be, a basic education for all could result in more economic success. A literate agricultural labour force and a skilled industrial body of workers are generally accepted as prerequisites for advancement.

In the early 1980s the Nicaraguan government, with assistance from Oxfam, the United Council of Churches and UNESCO, initiated an intensive literacy drive. A census located illiterate adults and potential teachers and then a pyramid system was employed to train them. An initial core of 80 teachers trained 560 new teachers and so on until nearly 100 000 new literacy teachers were ready. The campaign was promoted nationally through the media of radio, television and posters. Within 6

21

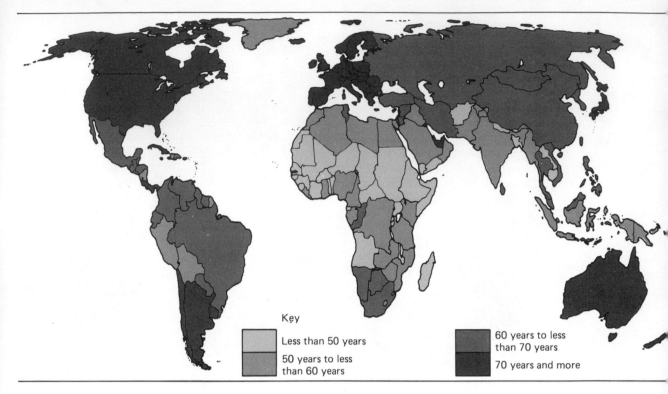

2.15 Life expectancy at birth – 1983

Key

Less than 50 years

50 years to less than 60 years

60 years to less than 70 years

70 years and more

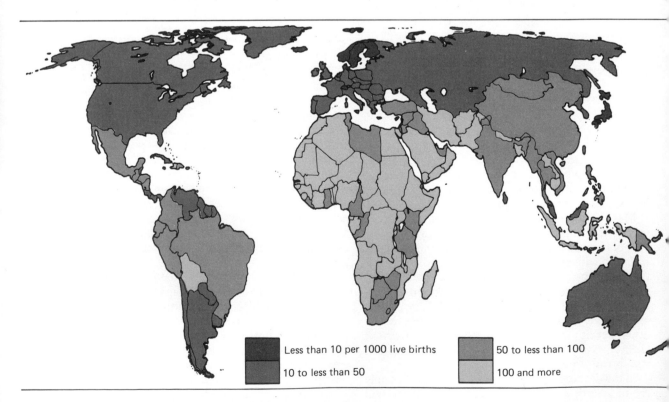

Less than 10 per 1000 live births

10 to less than 50

50 to less than 100

100 and more

2.16 Infant mortality rates – 1983

months more than half a million citizens completed a basic literacy programme. However, even the most successful campaign will fail without a follow-up scheme. The root cause of illiteracy, that is the lack of universal primary education, is now regarded as one of the fundamental priorities for development.

No attempt has been made so far to define illiterate. The dictionary describes it as, 'unable to read or write'. However the newspaper article on page 20 reveals an additional idea, that of 'functional illiteracy.'

A recent Gallup Poll in Britain suggested that 6 to 10% of the adult population in Britain are functionally illiterate. One of the tests used was a standard train timetable. Four out every ten adults failed to answer the basic questions.

Life expectancy

One of the biggest changes in human life during the last two decades is that people in developing countries can expect to live longer: 60 years for an infant born in 1984 compared with 45 years for an infant born in 1960. The corresponding increase for the industrial countries is to 76 years, from about 70 years. However a study of Fig. 2.15 reveals a marked variation among the developing countries. In a dozen or so of the richer ones, life expectancy at birth is 70 or more, the same as in the industrial countries in 1960. In a dozen or so of the poorer ones it is still less than 45 years. Surviving the first years of life makes a big difference in life expectancy. In a developing country in 1984, when a newborn infant could expect to live 60 years, a 5 year old could expect to live another 61 years.

Infant mortality

Many more infants die in the developing countries than in the developed countries. This is due mainly to impure drinking water and unsanitary living conditions. The diets of pregnant women, nursing mothers, and babies are also contributing factors. Poor nutrition and sanitation contribute to disease.

Added to this, the availability of health care is often inadequate. The infant mortality rate thus indicates the health, nutrition, access to medical care and other conditions in a country. As health conditions improve, the infant mortality rate usually declines and life expectancy increases.

Fig. 2.16 shows the wide range in mortality in the first year of life. According to the Population Reference Bureau, in 1985 Finland and Japan with infant mortality rates of 6 per 1000 were the lowest in the world, whilst in Afghanistan the rate was 205 per 1000 i.e. one baby in five dies within 12 months of birth.

13. Describe and explain the kind of population and social data which would be useful to a developing country's government if it was carrying out the following programme of improvement:
a) expansion of primary and secondary education;
b) extension of rural medical services;
c) flooding part of a river valley to provide a multi-purpose reservoir.

14. 'The problem in much of the third world today is not so much unemployment, or lack of work, but more a shortage of paid employment.' Discuss this statement with reference to any area you have studied.

15. The findings of the Gallop Poll and the newspaper article on functional illiteracy suggest that the data in Fig. 2.13 is subject to some doubt. How can it be possible for UNESCO and the World Development Report to state that less than 1% of the adult population in the U.S.A. and the U.K. are illiterate, when others indicate a totally different pattern?

16. Study Figs. 2.14, 2.15 and 2.16. What evidence is there to suggest that the world can be divided into three groups – the developed or advanced societies; the developing societies; and countries which would appear to be static as far as development is concerned?

3
Food and farming

'Feed the World' was the message from Bob Geldof and Band Aid in a highly successful campaign in 1985 which focused on the hunger facing millions in the African Sahel (Fig. 3.1). On first hearing this plea and on watching the television reports from Ethiopia that showed such terrible human suffering and starvation, it might have seemed that the worst fears of Thomas Malthus had been realised and that the world's population (4.8 billion in 1985) had truly exceeded available food supplies. However, the notion that the world might have a shortage of food was quashed by a 1986 World Bank Report on 'Poverty and Hunger' which stated very simply that 'the world has ample food'. Indeed, an official of the Food and Agriculture Organisation (F.A.O.) shortly afterwards estimated that the earth's resources could feed as many as 36 billion people, nearly seven times the present world population. How real, then, is the need to 'Feed the World' when farmers appear to produce ample food?

Production, consumption and nutrition

Approximately 98% of all human food is produced by farming, including **horticulture**. The remaining 2% comes from the sea. Plant production (crops) forms the basis of world agriculture and the most important primary agricultural products are the edible grasses – the grain or **cereal** crops. Only a handful of these plants provide almost all of the world's food crop, though at least 80 000 are thought to be edible. Cereal crops are consumed directly by people but they also form the raw foodstuff for the raising of animals. To meet minimum nutritional requirements, the world needs to produce an average of 2450 calories per person per day. This figure is based on a daily **calorie intake** of just under 1000 calories for each baby to over 3500 calories for an adult working person. Calorie requirements can, however, also vary according to other criteria such as sex, climatic conditions, height, weight and type of work being undertaken. In 1986 it was estimated that there was enough food

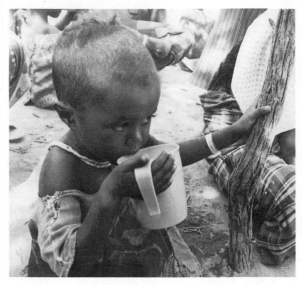

3.1 Refugee child at Jalalaksi Camp, Somalia

in the form of grain produced in the world to provide every person with over 3000 calories.

Grains generally form the main, sometimes the only, part of the protein intake in the diet of people in the poorer countries. However, as standards of living improve, as is evident in many of the richer countries, there is an increasing demand for a higher consumption of protein in the form of animal products, especially meat (see Fig. 3.2). It is the grain crops that form the basis of animal feedstuffs and, as a result, only 60% of the world's crops are actually eaten directly by humans, the rest being used to fatten livestock. To produce one unit of meat protein requires an average of eight units of vegetable protein (cereals) which could be consumed directly by humans. Also fish, an important source of protein, are not wholly consumed by humans since nearly half goes towards non-human consumptions such as producing animal feed and fertilizer. The average amount of cereals consumed annually per person varies greatly, therefore, between rich and poor countries (Fig. 3.3). Developed countries account for only 25% of the

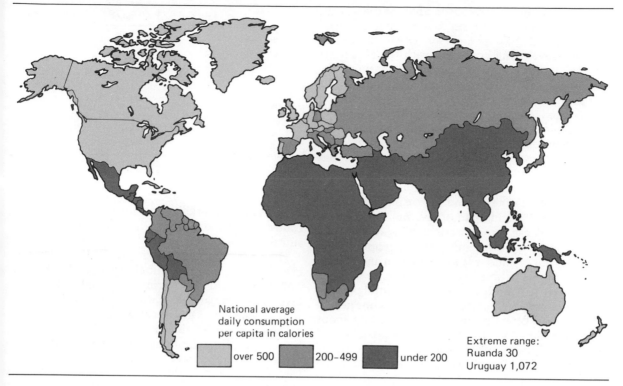

National average
daily consumption
per capita in calories

over 500 200–499 under 200

Extreme range:
Ruanda 30
Uruguay 1,072

3.2 Animal protein consumption

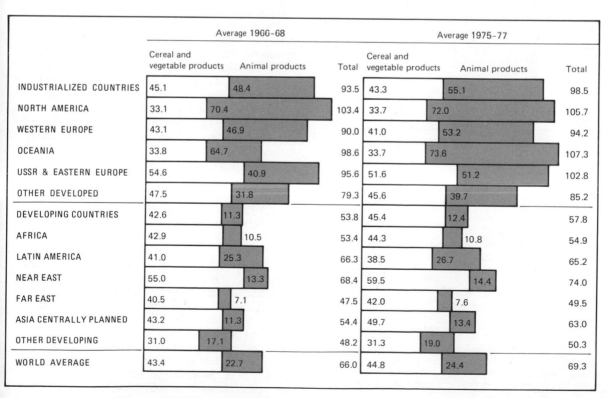

	Average 1966–68			Average 1975–77		
	Cereal and vegetable products	Animal products	Total	Cereal and vegetable products	Animal products	Total
INDUSTRIALIZED COUNTRIES	45.1	48.4	93.5	43.3	55.1	98.5
NORTH AMERICA	33.1	70.4	103.4	33.7	72.0	105.7
WESTERN EUROPE	43.1	46.9	90.0	41.0	53.2	94.2
OCEANIA	33.8	64.7	98.6	33.7	73.6	107.3
USSR & EASTERN EUROPE	54.6	40.9	95.6	51.6	51.2	102.8
OTHER DEVELOPED	47.5	31.8	79.3	45.6	39.7	85.2
DEVELOPING COUNTRIES	42.6	11.3	53.8	45.4	12.4	57.8
AFRICA	42.9	10.5	53.4	44.3	10.8	54.9
LATIN AMERICA	41.0	25.3	66.3	38.5	26.7	65.2
NEAR EAST	55.0	13.3	68.4	59.5	14.4	74.0
FAR EAST	40.5	7.1	47.5	42.0	7.6	49.5
ASIA CENTRALLY PLANNED	43.2	11.3	54.4	49.7	13.4	63.0
OTHER DEVELOPING	31.0	17.1	48.2	31.3	19.0	50.3
WORLD AVERAGE	43.4	22.7	66.0	44.8	24.4	69.3

3.3 Distribution of proteins in grammes per person per day

world's population yet consume half of the world's total cereal crops with an average annual cereal intake of 1017 kg per person. By comparison, poorer, developing countries, with three-quarters of the world's total population, consume the remainder at an average annual intake of 182 kg per person. Therefore, while increasing population has created an increase in demand for food, it has been the increase in individual consumption, both in the developed countries and in the fast growing urban centres of developing countries, that has contributed greatly to the world growth in food demand. In some developing countries this has meant an increasing dependence on imported grain during the 1980s in spite of economic stagnation and debt. These comparisons provide some of the clues as to why large numbers of people in the world go hungry and why **overnutrition** and **obesity** are nutritional problems among others.

Between 1970 and 1983 the world's total population increased by a quarter but over the same period of time total cereal production increased by about one third (Fig. 3.4). In developed, industrial countries cereal output rose three times as fast as population over the same twelve year period. Such agricultural production has given rise in E.E.C. countries, through the Common Agricultural Policy (**C.A.P.**), to surpluses of various food-stuffs – wine and milk lakes, butter and grain mountains (Fig. 3.5). Such surpluses have been the centre of much controversy. They are defended by

	1967–1971	1978	1982–1983
Sugar	82	125	159
Butter	91	118	114
Milk fat	100	112	119
Barley	103	112	112
Rye	100	108	98
Wine	97	107	104
Poultry	101	103	111
Soft Wheat	–	102	121
Beef	90	95	105

3.5 Self-sufficiency of the E.E.C. in agricultural products (%)

some as being desirable to ensure the availability of food supplies and to ensure that supplies reach consumers at reasonable prices.

However, food surpluses have also been criticised for having a destabilizing and depressing effect on world food prices, especially those of cereals, which can occur when food surpluses are sold off cheaply. They are also thought by some to be morally indefensible at a time when large numbers of people suffer **hunger** and **malnutrition**. In spite of the impressive overall growth of agricultural output worldwide, the picture is less impressive when per capita figures are concerned (Fig. 3.6). In many of the developing and least developed countries population growth rates are leading food production by a substantial rate. For example, total food production for the least developed countries increased by an average of 2.2% between 1971 and 1980 but production per head actually decreased. The situation is even more grim in Africa where the reduction in average food production per capita since 1970 and an increase in hunger has been brought about not only by population increase but by adverse climatic conditions such as those experienced in the Sahel countries such as Ethiopia and Sudan, civil strife and poor agricultural policies.

It is difficult to estimate how many hungry people there are in the world. Figures from the World Bank estimate that some 350 million people are so inadequately fed and suffer from undernutrition that their growth is stunted and their health is seriously endangered. They also calculate that over 700 million are seriously undernourished receiving too little to support even a minimum of physical activity let alone an active working life. F.A.O. estimates, although less specific, are more stark and pointed. They state that about one half of the world is badly fed, 10% suffer real starvation with one third of all children being malnourished. Indeed, it is the children who are particularly at risk. It has been estimated that at least 17 million of the 125 million children born in 1982 died of mal-

Region	Average Production		
	1960–1971	1972–1983	Change
	(1000 metric tons)		
AFRICA – rice	2 248	2 798	24.5
wheat/barley	5 661	7 251	28.1
sorghum/millets	14 069	17 302	23.0
maize	27 015	34 618	28.1
U.S.A.	181 982	265 022	45.6
CANADA	30 321	40 576	33.8
C. AMERICA – rice	642	912	42.1
maize	12 678	18 377	45.0
S. AMERICA – wheat/barley	19 439	26 234	35.0
rice	2 741	4 186	52.7
maize	18 222	28 402	55.9
OCEANIA – wheat/barley	13 149	18 311	39.3
S. ASIA – rice	18 798	23 347	24.2
wheat/barley	11 227	17 073	52.1
INDIA	74 752	104 000	39.1
E. ASIA – rice	35 505	50 798	43.1
N. ASIA – rice	19 832	17 620	−11.1
M. EAST – wheat/barley	23 699	31 681	33.7
EUROPE – wheat/barley	142 430	192 104	34.9
wheat/barley	30 509	44 644	46.3
U.S.S.R.	138 436	180 952	30.7
WORLD (excl. China)	829 215	1 133 902	36.7

3.4 World cereal production – 1960–83

	Change		Annual rate of change		
	1979–80	1980–81	1971–75	1976–80	1971–80
TOTAL FOOD PRODUCTION					
Market economies	3.1	3.9	3.2	2.5	3.2
Africa	4.1	2.0	1.7	1.8	1.7
Far East	3.6	6.0	3.4	2.4	3.4
Latin America	2.9	3.3	3.7	3.3	3.9
Near East	1.1	0.7	3.6	1.8	3.3
Asian centrally planned economies	−0.4	3.4	3.4	3.4	3.2
All developing countries	2.0	3.8	3.3	2.8	3.2
Least developed countries	5.1	0.8	2.8	2.3	2.2
PER CAPITA FOOD PRODUCTION					
Market economies	0.5	1.3	0.7	−0.2	0.6
Africa	1.0	−1.0	−1.1	−1.1	−1.2
Far East	1.1	3.5	1.0	−0.1	0.9
Latin America	0.2	0.6	1.0	0.6	1.2
Near East	−1.7	−2.1	0.9	−1.0	0.6
Asian centrally planned economies	−1.8	2.1	1.7	2.0	1.6
All developing countries	−0.3	1.5	1.0	0.5	1.0
Least developed countries	2.2	−2.0	0.4	−0.5	−0.4

3.6 Changes in total and per capita food production for crops and livestock in developing countries – 1971–80

nutrition and disease before they reached the age of 5. No matter how the numbers are estimated the outlook for the elimination of hunger in the world is not encouraging. Even the most optimistic figures in the F.A.O. study 'Agriculture: Toward 2000' suggests that there will be at least 260 million hungry people in the world by the end of the century.

What is it that brings about this apparent mismatch between population and food resources and what is being done about it? Some observers suggest that part of the problem lies in the colonial heritage of many poorer countries in which the traditional self-sufficient food patterns of growing staple crops such as rice, corn and root crops, were altered to that of commercial, **plantation** tea, cotton, rubber and coffee, thus developing cash crops at the expense of domestic food production.

However, the point must be made that some plantations, especially those of South East Asia, were established in sparsely settled areas and many of the original banana growing areas in central America were developed on land recovered from disease-infested swamps which lacked infrastructure and which national governments could not develop.

In spite of these arguments in favour of plantation farming, the introduction of crops such as sugar has been blamed as being one of the most serious disruptors to staple food production. This is perhaps best seen in Brazil which produced more than 2.6 million tonnes of sugar in 1982, making it the third largest single sugar producer in the world. At the same time, nearly three-quarters of the population in the North East region of Brazil, the main sugar growing area, were estimated to be suffering from malnutrition. A major problem in the growing of sugar cane is that it takes 16 months to grow a single sugar crop. This means that two or three crops of traditional staples such as rice are lost whenever a single sugar cane crop is grown. Add to this the need to change the irrigation system after each sugar crop and the result is a loss of nearly a half of the land available for food growing over a three year period.

Also blamed for food shortages today has been the introduction of coffee plantations. The introduction of such colonial plantations in Java over one hundred years ago is said to be still having an effect on the rural economy today. The initial coffee scheme failed because the area used was one of thin soils on top of limestone. The excessive removal of trees for the coffee plants led to rapid soil erosion which today means that only low protein cassava can be grown on the poor soils. This crop keeps the local people alive but only with a very poor quality of diet.

Colonial plantation farming is said to have caused another problem that can be seen in the African Sahel today. Here, French colonial rubber, cotton and peanut plantations replaced the traditional foods of millet and sorghum. By the 1930s there was such a shortage of staple foods and the threat of widespread hunger that the French imported large quantities of rice from Indo-China.

3.7 Child with kwashiorkor, the result of poor diet

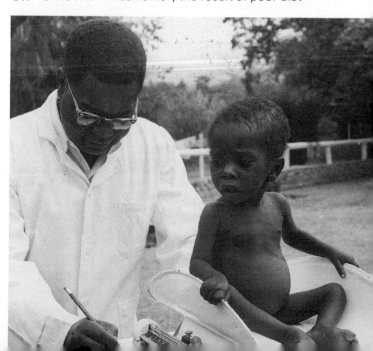

Today, most Africans in the area are so used to this rice that they have to import it in large quantities. One observer of this change stated that it was a sad irony that rice, needing so much water, has replaced drought-resistant millet and sorghum in the diets of people in one of the most drought-afflicted areas in the world.

Similarly, today the ownership of land in poor countries by foreign **transnational** companies growing plantation crops can lead to a lack of basic food production for human consumption. It is argued that such transnational activities limit agricultural development by limiting any diversification of the economy, create a dependence on the transnational company for a source of livelihood, cause underuse of farmland, and lessen the ability of farming to contribute to the country's industrial development since so many aspects of farming are in foreign hands. On the other hand, such foreign interests in farming do mean that the host country can gain from trade and distribution of the crops that are grown.

1. Why do you think the Band Aid campaign was so successful?

2. Describe and explain the patterns shown in Fig. 3.2.

3. Look at Fig. 3.3. Describe and account for the differences in intake of cereal/vegetable animal products (a) between developed and developing countries in 1977 and (b) within developed and developing countries between 1967 and 1977.

4. What are your views on the food surpluses produced by the countries of the E.E.C.?

5. Use your atlas to help you name the countries of the African Sahel.

6. Make a list of the advantages and disadvantages foreign, transnational companies can bring to an area of a developing country.

Food wastage

What aggravates the problems of the hungry is food spoilage and waste, something that is common to both rich and poor countries. In the U.K. it is estimated that as much as 25% of all food is lost through accident, theft or poor storage between leaving the farm and reaching the dinner table. In the case of perishables such as fruit and vegetables the loss is thought to be as high as 40%. In the countries of the third world, the F.A.O. calculate that up to 50% of all harvests can be lost. This may

be due to inefficient harvesting and threshing machinery, poor transportation, contamination and rotting through poor storage and to crops being wasted by rodents, birds and insects such as locusts. In addition to this is the food that is 'lost' through corruption, something which increases as food becomes scarcer. It is this corruption which can prevent food aid reaching the people most in need of it and which affords an excuse to some individuals and governments in the richer countries for not contributing or continuing to contribute to food aid through international agencies such as the U.N. and F.A.O.

One unfortunate trend that has emerged in many poor countries is that food wastage has increased as attempts have been made to increase food production. Part of this waste has come about because of the inability of stores and centres to handle such large additional amounts of food grains. Also, in some countries such as Bangladesh, much of an extra crop such as rice is harvested in the rainy season thus making post harvest losses, especially moulding, more likely. It is, therefore, not always traditional techniques of farming and storage facilities that contribute towards wastage of food in the poorer countries as is usually thought, but attempts to increase the volume of food production brought about by developments such as the **Green Revolution**.

Green Revolution

Since the mid-1960s agricultural scientists have introduced new crops and farming methods through biochemical and mechanical innovation to increase crop yields in developing countries. The idea behind this 'Green Revolution' has been that by boosting food production, food shortages would decrease, health would improve, more jobs would be created on the land and that any food surpluses would be marketed so that investment in farming and industrial development might commence (see Fig. 3.8). There can be little doubt that the various farming techniques and policies, together with the resultant social changes, have had success in some areas of the poor world and among some crops. However, it has also been criticised as a failure and a major factor in making some people in the third world even more destitute.

During the 1940s and 1950s attempts were made to develop a **high yielding variety (H.Y.V.)** of wheat which could be grown with the help of fertilizer and irrigation to dramatically increase the crop yield for a given area in third world countries. The H.Y.V. Mexipak wheat that was developed

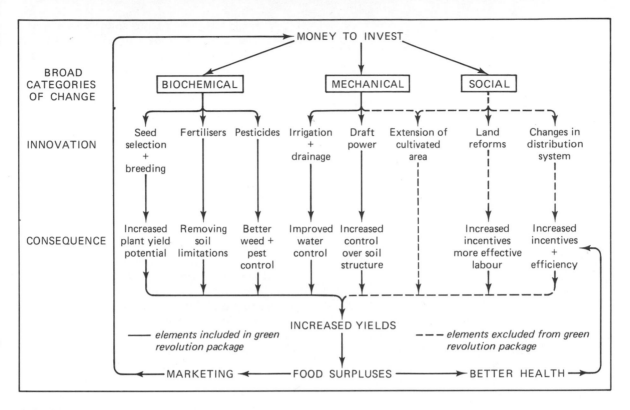

3.8 Choices in agricultural change

3.9 Green Revolution, Pakistan. On the right, no fertilizer has been used.

	Wheat 1961–5	1981	Rice 1961–5	1981
India	850	1650	1500	2000
China	900	1950	2800	4250
Japan	2300	3050	5000	5650
U.S.A.	1700	2300	4400	5450
Mexico	2100	3500	2300	3150
U.K.	4000	5500	–	–

* 'Yield' is defined as the amount of a crop produced on a given area of land: in this case, the weight in kilogrammes produced from one crop grown on a hectare of land.

3.10 Average cereal yields for selected countries (yields kg/ha)

was a dwarf variety which converted fertilizer efficiently into food grain rather than into stalk or leaves and which did not topple over with weight. The H.Y.V. wheat, which produced four times the yield of traditional wheats, helped Mexico to become self-sufficient in wheat whereas only fifteen years earlier the country had to import over half of her grain. At the same time, H.Y.V. rice seeds were developed by the International Rice Research Institute of the Philippines (I.R.R.I.), the best known being I.R.8 rice and more recently I.R.28 and I.R.36. The effect these new H.Y.V. seeds had on food yields was dramatic. Rice production in Sri Lanka and Pakistan increased by over a third between 1966 and 1968 and in most countries where the new H.Y.V. seeds were adopted – Mexico, India, Thailand, Korea, Indonesia and the Philippines – there was a 20%–35% increase in yields over the traditional strains. Worldwide, the area under H.Y.V. crops increased from 40 000 acres in 1964 to over 35 million acres a decade later (Fig. 3.10). However, adoption of the

	1966	1978
INDIA		
Wheat	4%	71%
Sorghum	1%	19%
Rice	2.5%	42%
BANGLADESH		
Boro rice	26%	65%
Aus rice	0.5%	15%
Aman rice	0.2%	16%
PAKISTAN		
Wheat	16%	75%
Rice	0.2%	45%

3.11 Adoption of high yielding varieties (% of total crop)

H.Y.V. seeds has varied from country to country with considerably less impact in Africa and Latin America than in Asia. It has also varied from region to region and even from crop to crop. For example, in India, the 'Revolution' has been confined largely to Punjab and Haryana states with wheat, and to a lesser extent, rice being the main crops involved. The introduction of these new seeds has meant that food production has been able to keep pace with population growth in some areas since the mid-1960s (Fig. 3.11). It has allowed some individuals, areas and countries to become self-sufficient in food supplies with surpluses earning valuable revenue through sales at local, national and international markets. In some areas, the new varieties, together with faster land preparation and harvesting due to mechanization, have allowed 'double cropping' or even 'triple cropping' where irrigation is available since the new crops mature in a much shorter time (100–130 days) than traditional varieties which could take up to six months to mature. This **multiple cropping**, which produces more food from any given land area, has eased the pressure of population on the land and cut down on the need to migrate from rural areas because of food shortages. The H.Y.V. crops have also led to an increase in employment opportunities in some of the areas where they are introduced. The crops demand considerably more labour inputs than traditional varieties as they need careful planting, regular applications of fertilizer, insecticides, constant weeding and carefully managed irrigation. A further advantage brought about by the adoption of H.Y.V. seeds has been that seasonal unemployment is eliminated. The constant caring for the crops and the multiple cropping has evened out the demands for labour thus providing all year round employment for farmers in some areas.

Disadvantages of the Green Revolution

There have, however, been problems with the adoption of the Green Revolution technology. Initially, some of the new crops produced from the H.Y.V. seeds were not to the taste of the people eating them. For example, in northern India, the early H.Y.V. wheat did not make good chapatis (discs of bread eaten in that area). However, further research has produced varieties of most seeds that lead to customer satisfaction.

The H.Y.V. seeds perform best on fertile soils with ample supplies of water and fertilizer to ensure the return of a high yield. Where such inputs are inadequate or not correctly managed, a 'yield gap' can emerge with the H.Y.V. seed yielding a smaller actual crop than its potential, producing, in some cases, little more food than traditional seeds. Since the H.Y.V. crops have a short stalk, careful management of water and irrigation is also necessary to ensure that crops do not drown. Initially the need for irrigation meant that drier areas with rain-fed farming could not grow the early H.Y.V. crops and the impact of the new techology was limited to irrigated areas such as the R. Indus complex in India and Pakistan, the Tigris/Euphrates valley in the Middle East and other irrigated areas. This has changed recently as H.Y.V. seeds, for example cassava, that are suitable for use in drier areas, have been successfully developed and are now being grown. However, the development of coarse cereals such as millet and maize on which many of the very poorest farmers in the world depend has been less touched by the new seed technology. Also, there has been a dramatic change away from growing pulses such as beans, peas and lentils, which provide much-needed protein, to many poor people, to more profitable H.Y.V. wheat.

In areas where large quantities of water have been needed for the new H.Y.V. crops, electric pumps and **tubewells** have been installed to lift the water into the fields. Such has been the huge number of pumps installed, in areas such as Uttar Pradesh in India, that the water table has dropped so much that only the very deepest tubewells can reach it, leaving the shallower wells dry. This has greatly affected the smaller farmer who cannot afford deeper wells and has even contributed to soil erosion. Poor management of irrigation water has also led to salinisation and waterlogging as salts are lifted into the root zone of crops. In the Punjab, irrigation water seeping into the ground has raised the water table by up to 9 metres in as many years. In India as a whole, it has been estimated that as much as 15% of all irrigated land has been damaged by salinity with the figures as high as 20% in Pakistan and 25% in Iraq.

Another factor associated with the Green Revolution which has led to soil erosion has been the move away from traditional non-mechanical to mechanised cultivation. The intensive nature of the new farming techniques together with the clearance of forest and other vegetation can eventually weaken the soil structure and this, together with the greater incidence of post-harvest burning of stubble, can lead to soil erosion as has been the case in schemes centred on the Sokoto-Rima, Kano River and Chad basins in northern Nigeria.

The actual cost of introducing irrigation, machinery and fertilizers has, however, meant that the benefits of the Green Revolution have not been reaped by all farmers in the third world. The costs involved have meant that the debt owed by farmers has increased and it is felt by some that many of the developments are too dependent on imported 'western' technology and expertise that is inappropriate to the farming systems of developing countries. As a result, few farmers can afford these expensive inputs or the repayments for the adoption of the technology necessary to participate in the Green Revolution and thus increase food production. Therefore, in many areas, it has been the wealthier 'credit worthy' farmers and landlords who have participated in the various new farming schemes, being able to buy or borrow money for the necessary seeds, fertilizers, insecticides, irrigation and additional wages for labour. It has, therefore, tended to be larger landowning farmers who have seen improved yields and profits while landless labourers, tenants and **sharecroppers**, with little or no title to the land they work, have benefited least. In some cases, increased profits have allowed landowners to buy or lease land from smaller, poorer farmers, thus forcing them off the land. For example, in Sonora state, Mexico the average farm size before the Green Revolution was 400 acres. After 20 years of the new scheme it had climbed to 2000 acres with many smaller farmers having been bought over. The increased food production from the land has also led to an increase in the value of the land. In the Indian Punjab land values have jumped three to five times in the Green Revolution areas and the greater certainty of high yields and profits provided by the new technology has led to a reduction in the need for some landowners to share risk with sharecroppers. As a result, some sharecroppers have seen their role change, being retained only as farm labourers by the landowner.

In other countries, especially India in the 1970s, the non-distribution to the peasant farmers of extra profits brought about by increased yields led to violent conflicts between landlords and their farm workers with many killings. These bloody incidents, such as in Thanjavur district, Tamil Nadu on 26 December 1968, led one observer to question whether the Green Revolution was not really turning into a 'Red Revolution'.

In some parts of the third world, the introduction of machinery and new technology has improved the productivity of the land and has created many new jobs. However, the Green Revolution has, in some parts, actually been responsible for the loss of farming jobs. In such areas the machinery, especially the tractor, has replaced the abundant manual labour in the various stages of food production from ploughing and sowing to irrigation and harvesting. A study in Pakistan suggests that each tractor introduced has destroyed an average of five manual farming jobs. This loss of jobs has been especially high in the non-rice growing areas since rice is much less suited to tractor mechanisation than most other grain crops. At this point it is interesting to note the impact the technology and change associated with the Green Revolution has had on women. Studies in India suggest that among some of the richer peasants the new farming system with its increased income is seen as evidence of improved family prestige and, therefore, women 'withdraw' voluntarily from direct involvement in farming. However, in the poorer peasant households and among landless labourers, women have been forcibly 'squeezed' out of their farm jobs through the introduction of mechanization with a resultant increase in poverty and destitution. In some cases, the new technology has considerably increased the workload for women. For example, mechanised ploughing may simply mean longer hours and harder work for women as might the need for increased amounts of water collected (usually done by women) to mix with pesticides and fertilizers. An F.A.O. report perhaps best sums up the effect of the Green Revolution on women by saying that 'decisions on whether or how quickly to introduce technology are almost never in women's hands . . . women seem to be pitted against technological progress'.

A further problem arising from the use of the H.Y.V. crops of the Green Revolution has been the fact that they have proved to be much more susceptible to disease, pests and drought than the traditional lower yielding varieties. Concern has been expressed, for example, that the great grain-lands of the Indus basin could be wiped out by one strain of disease particularly deadly to the wheat type planted there. Such a tragedy almost occurred in Europe a hundred years ago when almost every European vineyard was destroyed by an insect living on the vines' roots. Fortunately, the North American vine was immune to it and European wines were saved by being grafted on to North American roots. In Korea the unusually wet, cool summer of 1980 showed that its H.Y.V. rice had little tolerance to cold conditions. As a result, Korea fell below self-sufficiency in its staple grain and had to import, at great expense, huge quantities of rice from Japan.

The early H.Y.V. rices such as I.R.8 were highly susceptible to bacterial blight, fungus, leaf hoppers and stem borers, necessitating high inputs of costly chemical insecticides and pesticides to ensure any

yield at all. Over the years new seeds have been developed that are more resistant to such ills but many still need expensive chemicals that are beyond the means of most peasant farmers to ensure healthy growth.

A recent development designed to eliminate total crop failure in H.Y.V. crops has taken place in India. 'Multiline' varieties of wheat seed have been developed to produce plants that look identical but comprise a dozen slightly different strains. The idea is that any particular wheat disease kills only a few of these strains so that a farmer risks losing only a small part, and not all, of his crop in a plague. Scientists have also developed kinds of crops that are less tasty to insects. In trials, how-ever, it has been found that such crops merely encourage the insects to go and eat the produce from a neighbouring farmer. More promising has been the research into varieties that practice 'peace-ful co-existence', producing grain even when pests have destroyed their leaves or developing diseases so slowly that the plant is not affected until after harvest time. Many of these technological develop-ments are still in their infancy and have had only limited effect on farming in the poor world although they do hold out some hope for the future. So too does the development of grain crops capable of producing their own fertilizer, like beans do at present. Such a breakthrough would remove one major barrier to participation by all in the Green Revolution – that of purchasing expen-sive and necessary fertilizer. Trials in developing such crops are still in their early stages and it is hoped that self-fertilizing grain crops will be avail-able by the end of this century. At the same time, development continues in the production of H.Y.V. seeds with even higher resistance to pests and diseases.

Food – the future

In an attempt to cut down on the feeding of valu-able grain as fodder to animals, techniques have been developed in which fodder can be made from petroleum. In this process, paraffin is fed to bacteria to produce a high protein edible powder which can be fed to animals. Algae, such as Chlorella, have been successfully cultivated to pro-duce a high protein material which, when dried, can be used for animal and human food. Much pro-gress has also been made in **hydroponics**. This tech-nique involves the growing of plants in water, sand or gravel without soil. Soluble plant food is fed to the plants and, under controlled temperature con-ditions, high yields of crops can be obtained with the added advantage of having no weeds or pests. The use of soyabean protein to produce artificial meat which has a higher protein content than real beef or pork is becoming more common and its further development holds considerable potential for lower 'real meat' demands, lower 'meat' prices and improved diets in the future. Considerable optimism has also been expressed at developments underway in extracting more food from the sea, obtaining food or animal feed from wood and leaves and using non-plant sources such as solar and other energy sources to allow amino acids to be produced which can then be used to fortify food. The consequences of such food developments could be enormous and may even eventually reduce the world's total dependence on farming as we know it today.

Conclusion

In spite of these many developments and the potential they may hold for the future of world food production, the fact remains that many millions of people in the world today are underfed, undernourished and dying of starvation. It is perhaps ironic that such a situation exists when the world as a whole, most nations in general and sizeable numbers of the population in particular are richer than at any other time in the history of mankind on this planet.

As has been seen, much work has and is being done, with varying degrees of success, in an attempt to reduce and eradicate world hunger. The Green Revolution has greatly increased food yields in some areas of the poor world. Also developments such as India's **White Revolution**, in which dairy farming schemes have been promoted, have gone some way towards improving the quality of diet for some. However, hunger and malnutrition are not removed by providing food supplies alone. The Brandt Report states 'the problem of hunger has to be faced as a part of domestic economic development and in its links with the international economy'. This suggests, firstly, the need to attack hunger at a local level by investing directly in appropriate farming developments which may include irrigation, crop storage, H.Y.V. seeds, land reform and the more equitable distribution of the benefits amongst all the farming people. Secondly, the statement suggests that there is a need for the richer countries of the North to recognise the links in the world economy and the influences they have on world food production, consumption, prices and trade. Also, the richer countries of the North must develop and expand their supportive roles to the poorer countries through continued scientific research, finance and food aid aimed not only at alleviating short term hunger but in helping mobilise the poor into raising agricultural production and building rural infrastructure for the longer term benefit of all.

7. Describe some of the examples of how food is wasted in your own country and how the wastage might be overcome.

8. Briefly outline the need for the Green Revolution.

9. With reference to Fig. 3.8, explain the methods involved in implementing the Green Revolution.

10. Discuss the statement that 'experience has shown that, in some cases, the expected degree of improvement in farming has not been achieved, while, in others, new problems have arisen'.

4

Health, disease and development

A non-Geographer looking through this book, may wonder why Geographers should study, 'Health and Disease.' Surely such a theme cannot be Geography? We shall see.

A person's health is related to a number of factors principally: a) environmental, and b) social and human factors. There are links between certain diseases and population distribution, density and wealth. Disease (or morbidity as it is known in medical statistics) obviously affects death rates, and life expectancy. A country with low health care provision is unlikely to have a firm base for economic growth and development.

Classification of disease

One method of classifying a disease relates to the overall prevalence of disease in an area. Certain diseases are always associated with particular areas. Tourists from Britain flying to Gambia will have to visit their doctor prior to departure, since malaria is present there, and precautions have to be taken. Such a disease can be labelled **endemic** i.e. a disease habitually present in an area due to permanent local causes.

Tourists flying to Italy would not normally expect to contract cholera. It is not endemic to Italy. However on occasion there may be a sudden outbreak . . . an **epidemic**, defined as, 'prevalent among a community at a special time, and produced by some causes not generally present in the area.' Other examples of epidemic diseases would include a wave of influenza striking Britain.

Endemic diseases are very often linked to environmental conditions, where disease carrying organisms can thrive without hindrance. It is possible for an endemic disease to spread to another area, thereby becoming epidemic. Air travel allows infected individuals to travel around the world very quickly, spreading disease. An infected person can be in Lagos in the morning and be in London that evening. Such **jet-borne** diseases can present a risk sometimes to the new community by introducing new diseases such as Lassa fever, cholera and typhoid.

When an epidemic disease spreads across a vast geographic area, as happened with 'Asian flu' in 1978, the word **pandemic** applies.

Endogenous and exogenous disease

An **endogenous** disease is one which is non-infectious and traditionally associated with the lifestyle of people in the developed world. Such diseases, which include cancers, bronchitis and heart disorders, pose no threat to non affected persons in the community.

Exogenous diseases are infectious or contagious whereby the disease producing organism can spread to other individuals.

Health care and provision must vary accordingly. For endogenous diseases, treatment or prevention is often linked to changing lifestyle, and is often aimed at the individual. A person with heart disease needs to adapt his or her habits. Drugs or surgery can supplement this action. Exogenous diseases tend to affect communities with treatment and prevention often involving massive community programmes.

Nutrition, health and development

'There is no drug to solve hunger, still less a vaccine to prevent it. . . .' (World Health Organization) Good health and sanitation tends to be taken for granted, and it is very easy to forget that high standards are not possible for many people. The requirements for a healthy life can, in theory, be simple to achieve: a balanced diet to ensure healthy growth and resistance to infection; pure water supplies to avoid the dangers from water-borne diseases: good quality housing; an organized and effective health care service.

However for many low income countries, the progress towards a healthy society is now slowly taking place, and people are living longer, with far fewer infants dying in the first years of life.

There are two groups of food related diseases: starvation and malnutrition.

Starvation, or **undernutrition** is essentially not having enough to eat. Carbohydrates, proteins and fats all provide the energy that is needed. The energy value of food is measured in **calories**, and the needs of a person vary according to sex, age, physique, work and climate. The average daily calorific intake of a healthy adult is in the region of 2500. Growing teenagers, or adults involved in hard physical employment may need closer to 4000.

As can be seen from Fig. 4.1, there are considerable spatial differences with regards to calorific intake. What this map does not show are the variations within countries. For example the South East of Brazil has a relatively higher standard of living, with higher income and levels of food intake than the poorer North East or inland areas.

According to the BRANDT REPORT, world food production in the period 1950 to 1980 rose annually by approximately $2\frac{1}{2}\%$. However, food demand during the same period grew by an annual average of just under 3%. Undernutrition by itself retards physical development, limits work potential and, when combined with malnutrition, causes an early death.

Malnutrition results when the diet is unbalanced and deficient in one or more of the three main food groups essential in a healthy diet:

a) protein, such as contained in meat, eggs, and milk;

b) carbohydrates, such as in cereals, sugar, fats, meat, eggs and potatoes;

c) minerals and vitamins, which are present in dairy produce, fruit, fish, vegetables meat and eggs.

It is possible to suffer from malnutrition, yet apparently have adequate food in quantity to keep going. A lack of any of these three essential foods can result in a number of **diet deficiency** diseases, such as kwashiorkor, marasmus or scurvy.

Once caught up in this downward spiral (see Fig. 4.3) it becomes very difficult to break free. Poor health results in reduced work rates, little scope for development, and under use of resources as well as immense human suffering.

1. Briefly describe the patterns shown in Fig. 4.1. What relationships can be seen between this map, and Figs. 2.14, 2.15 and 2.16? How much reliance can be placed with regard to the calorie intake information for South America?

2. Study Fig. 4.3 showing the downward spiral of health problems. In your own words explain what is shown.

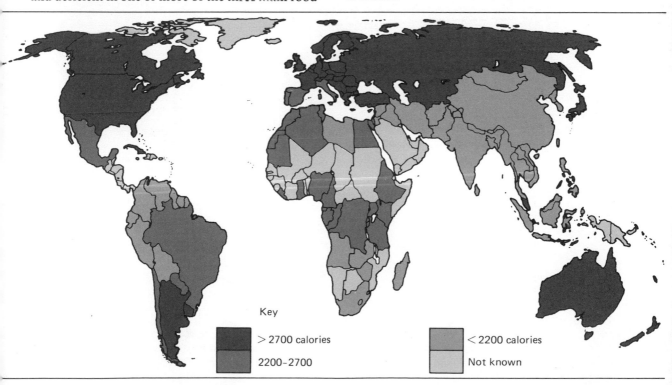

Key

■ > 2700 calories

■ 2200-2700

■ < 2200 calories

■ Not known

4.1 Calorie intake per person per day

Disease	Reason and symptoms	Social importance	Prevention	Locations
Kwashiorkor	Protein deficiency. Growth retarded. Bloated stomach. Hair changes colour, and may fall out. Apathetic.	Particularly distressing to see young people affected. Reduces potential work rate.	Well balanced diet. Milk, eggs, fish, meat, pulses, cheese. Various synthetic mixes used with success.	S.E. Asia; Central and West Africa.
Marasmus	Severe calorie deficiency as well as protein. Growth retarded, with severe wasting of skin and muscle. Vomiting and diarrhoea.	Again main target . . . the child. Frequently results in death.	Breast milk, cereals fats and oils. Synthetic formula of amino acids, glucose, salt and water.	S.E. Asia, Central and West Africa.
Beri-beri	Deficiency of vitamin B. Wasting and paralysis of limbs. Skin flakes, a diet with too much de-husked rice.	Affects adults as well as children. Ability to work greatly reduced. Also affects chronic alcoholics.	Balanced diet, with thiamine, a constituent part of vitamin B.	South and East Asia.
Pellagra	Deficiency of vitamin B, caused by lack of the niacin constituent resulting in diarrhoea, dementia (mental illness) and dermatitis.	Reduces ability to work. A country with many people suffering with Pellagra will not reach full development potential.	Well balanced diet, high in niacin. Health education.	Maize eating countries e.g. Italy, South Africa.
Night blindness	Severe vitamin A deficiency. Dry skin, kidney infection, respiratory problems. Inability to see at night. May lead to blindness, due to corneal ulcers.	The United Nations estimate that 1/2 million young children are infected each year. 2/3rd die within weeks.	Breast milk, carrots, fruit, fish, egg yolk, dairy produce. General health education.	S. and S.E. Asia; Latin America. West Africa.
Anaemia	Iron deficiency, pale complexion fatigue, loss of appetite, indigestion, and a cause of death in childbirth.	Particularly hits young adult women. Reduces ability to work.	Meat (especially liver), fruits and green vegetables.	South and S.E. Asia, Latin America, C. and W. Africa.
Rickets	Lack of vitamin D. Debilitating but not fatal. Legs and pelvis deformed. 'Swaddling' of babies should be avoided.	Affects babies and children. Deformation limits mobility and work potential.	Health education balanced diet, especially when pregnant. Cod liver oil, butter, and sunshine.	South Asia. Formerly common in Britain.
Scurvy	Lack of vitamin C. Gums bleed, hair and teeth fall out. Internal bleeding. Anaemia develops. Low resistance to infection.	Reduces work potential. Those suffering likely to catch further infections.	Fresh fruit, vegetables and sunshine.	Formerly common with sailors. Found still with single older people in developed countries, C. and W. Africa.

4.2 Major diet deficiency disease

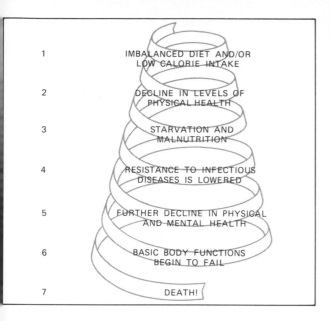

1	IMBALANCED DIET AND/OR LOW CALORIE INTAKE
2	DECLINE IN LEVELS OF PHYSICAL HEALTH
3	STARVATION AND MALNUTRITION
4	RESISTANCE TO INFECTIOUS DISEASES IS LOWERED
5	FURTHER DECLINE IN PHYSICAL AND MENTAL HEALTH
6	BASIC BODY FUNCTIONS BEGIN TO FAIL
7	DEATH!

4.3 Spiral of malnutrition and disease

growing reliance on powdered milk substitute, have resulted in making the problem more acute. Most food is cooked communally in some societies, is highly spiced and often based on vegetable protein. The outcome of this lack of appropriate and separate food for young children is often kwashiorkor, or indeed even more severe disease.

Prevention of kwashiorkor is, in the long term, more advantageous than attempting to cure it. Health education, either initiated by the individual governments, or by outside agencies such as the World Health Organization (W.H.O.), offers a way forward. Education on the value of a balanced diet and suitable food for babies is vital to ensure long term development. In severely drought affected areas such as the Sudan and Ethiopia, the W.H.O. has observed the success of using synthetic formulas containing a package of essential amino acids, glucose, an appropriate salt mixture and water on young children. Such a mixture has to be given in small amounts up to 10 times a day.

Fig. 4.2 is a summary table showing the main diet deficiency diseases, reasons for, symptoms, social importance, prevention and geographical locations.

3. Explain what is meant by the terms:
   endemic, epidemic, and pandemic.
   Give one example of each.

4. Explain the difference, with examples, between malnutrition and undernutrition.

5. 'The quality of foodstuff is as important as the quantity.' Comment on the validity of this statement with reference to Central and West Africa.

Case study: Kwashiorkor

In 1932 a British doctor in Ghana identified a disease in young children due to protein deficiency. The name given was a local tribal name, kwashiorkor. The common characteristics included growth failure, oedema (a watery unhealthy fat forms causing a distended stomach), diarrhoea, a fatty liver and death, if untreated. Affected children appear to be miserable, uninterested in food and seemingly apathetic regarding their future. If a child's mother is unhealthy and suffers from malnutrition, then the baby's physical and mental development will be retarded. Social customs may make it difficult for a young child to get enough protein. Early weaning from the breast, and the

WHO drive on blindness in children

The World Health Organization is launching a campaign against a disease described as 'a scourge shameful for mankind'. It is xerophthalmia blindness caused by vitamin A deficiency due to inadequate diet, which afflicts more than 500 000 young children each year in Africa, Asia and parts of Latin America.

Two-thirds of them die within weeks of becoming blind. Another six to seven million children, with less severe deficiencies, are very susceptible to severe respiratory infections and diarrhoea, often resulting in death.

The organization's programme will cost about $6 million (£4.2 million) annually.

Prevention consists of giving a child a capsule costing 2 US cents every six months. The rest of the money will be used for training local health care workers and in getting the message over to rural societies, that this is a disease easy to prevent and, in its early stages to cure.

In some countries – Ruanda and Burundi being notable examples – fruit, vegetables and small animals rich in vitamin A were available but few people ate them because of traditional prejudices.

4.4 Article from *The Times*, 11.10.85

Some concluding comments

Food related diseases are generally linked to countries with low income, limited educational development and insufficient cash resources. Food problems are currently endemic in large areas of South and South East Asia, Central and West Africa, Latin and South America. Conditions are always aggravated during drought, (as in the south Sahara fringe in the mid 1980s) or civil war (as in Nigeria in the 1970s.)

Diet related diseases can debilitate a person and can often be fatal, especially in children. Over 40% of all deaths in less developed areas are among children under 5 years. Such diseases also weaken the overall resistance of the human body making the effect of other diseases far more acute. For example, in the Gambia the mortality rate from measles, if unaccompanied by malnutrition, is 2.5%, whilst the rate from measles in children with malnutrition is nearer 20%.

The Brandt Report of 1980 calculated that 40% of pre-school children in low income areas exhibit clinical signs of malnutrition. To be positive, that 60% of such an age grouping do not show signs of malnutrition is a reflection of the success of health education programmes in many countries of the third world. Much work has yet to be done, but that work is underway. (See Fig. 4.4.)

6. With reference to Fig. 4.3 and the case study, kwashiorkor, suggest how the spiral of malnutrition and disease can be broken.

7. Referring to Fig. 4.5, which shows a list of major infectious diseases, draw up a list showing those diseases which you or your family have suffered from. Now draw up a second list showing those diseases a child in tropical West Africa might contract. Comment on your findings.

Infectious diseases

Causes

Fig. 4.5 lists the world's major **infectious** diseases, their causes and treatment. The main groups, identified by cause, are:

1. **Bacteria**, commonly found in every healthy body, can occasionally be harmful, and produce poisonous toxins which damage vital body organs. Such bacteria are associated with diseases like cholera, venereal disease, pneumonia and leprosy.
2. **Viruses** exist inside body cells, are extremely small and, since they multiply rapidly, can result in extensive damage very quickly. This group contains some of the world's most feared diseases.

Disease	Cause and transmitting vector	Treatment	Prevention	Occurrence
Influenza	Virus; airborne droplets		Immunization	Worldwide
Measles	Virus; human contact		Immunization	Worldwide
Poliomyelitis	Virus; contact, droplets, food		Immunization	Worldwide
Rabies	Virus; animal bite		Early immunization	Almost worldwide
Rubella	Virus; contact		Immunization	Worldwide
Smallpox	Virus; contact		Immunization	Now eradicated
Yellow Fever	Virus; mosquito bite		Immunization	Tropical world
Bubonic Plague	Bacteria: rat flea bite	Antibiotics	Hygiene, immunization	Rarely occurs
Cholera	Bacteria (Vibrio); contact water and food	Saline drip Antibiotics	Hygiene, immunization	Africa, Asia S.E. Europe
Gonorrhoea	Bacteria (diplococcus); contact	Antibiotics		Worldwide
Leprosy	Bacteria (bacillus) contact	Drugs	Medical screening	Tropical world
Pneumonia	Bacteria (diplococcus); air	Antibiotics		Worldwide
Tuberculosis	Bacteria (bacillus); contact, milk	Antibiotics	Immunization	Worldwide
Typhoid	Bacteria (bacillus); food, water	Antibiotics	Hygiene, immunization	Poor hygiene
Amoebic Dysentery	Protozoan (amoeba); food, water	Drugs	Hygiene, education	Poor hygiene
Elephantiasis	Metazoan (filaria); mosquito	Drugs, surgery	Hygiene, education	Tropical world
Malaria	Protozoan (plasmodium) mosquito	Drugs	Drugs, education	Now tropical
Sleeping Sickness	Protozoan (trypanosome) Tsetse fly	Drugs	Eradicate flies	Tropical Africa
Typhus	Rickettsia; louse or flea bite	Antibiotics	Hygiene, immunization	Inter tropical
Schistosomiasis or Bilharzia	Worms; snails and water	Drugs	Hygiene, education Mass campaigns	Tropical world
Onchocerciasis or River blindness	Worms; Simulium blackfly	Drugs	Mass campaigns	Tropical Africa

4.5 Selected infectious diseases, causes and treatment

3. **Protozoa** attack the blood supply by damaging red cells. Malaria and trypanosomiasis are two widespread tropical diseases.

Parasitic fleas, ticks, lice or worms survive by living on and from another living organism. This **host** can be either human or animal. For example the flea bug is a parasite which lives on rats and is responsible for bubonic plague. There are a variety of ways in which a disease can enter the body. Direct contact can result in infection. However, for many other diseases, a **vector** is required. A vector is any living carrier (insect, snail, rat) of an infectious disease. The carrier itself is not harmed by the disease yet, on contact with humans, the disease is transmitted.

Case study: diseases linked to poor hygiene

Leprosy

Several years ago lepers were outcasts forced to wear a bell around their necks, so that 'clean' people could hear them coming and run in case they caught the disease. Even today, in Nepal, lepers are not allowed to hold public office. Leprosy is still an endemic disease in many areas of the tropical world, with nearly 14 million people affected. (About 8 million live in South Asia.) Of these only one-quarter receive effective medical treatment. The W.H.O. has been studying and working on the problem of leprosy for many years. If untreated, leprosy is a horrific disease which can permanently cripple, disfigure and even blind a victim. The cause of leprosy is a micro-organism similar to the tuberculosis bacillus. There are a number of different forms of leprosy, but two are contagious. The incubation period can be as long as five years, and it is possible to be a carrier, without displaying any visible evidence of the disease.

With backing from the World Bank, the W.H.O. is tackling leprosy on several fronts. There is a search for new drugs, since the micro-organism is growing increasingly resistant to Dapsone, the drug used at present in mass campaigns. Treatment with Dapsone can now vary from six months to a lifetime, so in the Cuttack area of India new drugs, which will have shorter treatment schedules, are being pioneered. Vaccines to prevent the disease and tests for early infection are also being developed.

Contrary to popular opinion, leprosy is still very active; however, the W.H.O. has improved the situation significantly, and people who now contract leprosy can lead fairly normal lives, and can contribute to the development of their communities.

Cholera

Cholera is the classic epidemic disease of the 19th century, caused by a bacterium spread through the faeces of infected people. It is caught by drinking polluted water or eating contaminated food. Originally cholera was endemic in India, but with increased trading, migration and improved transport, it spread to epidemic proportions throughout Asia and the Western Hemisphere. There have been seven worldwide pandemics, the last one reaching Britain in 1970. (See Fig. 4.6 showing the cholera life cycle and control.)

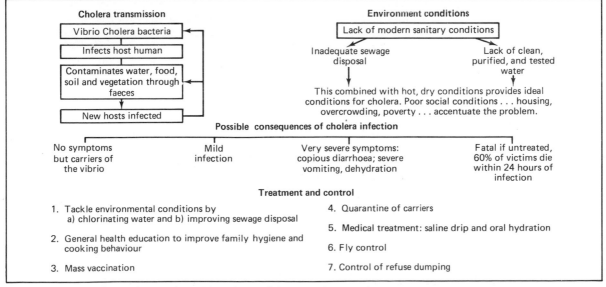

4.6 Cholera: life cycle, environmental conditions and control

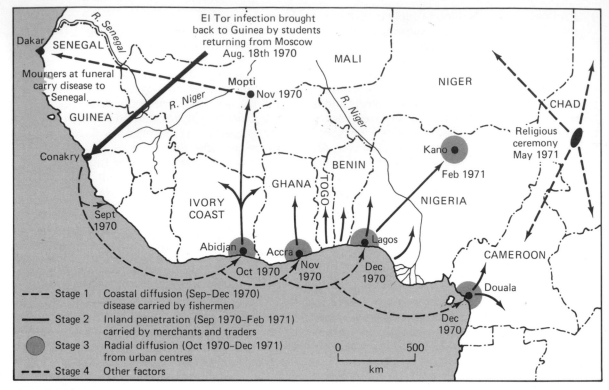

4.7 Diffusion of cholera in W. Africa – 1970–71

Map labels:
- Dakar, SENEGAL
- R. Senegal
- El Tor infection brought back to Guinea by students returning from Moscow Aug. 18th 1970
- MALI
- NIGER
- CHAD
- Mourners at funeral carry disease to Senegal
- Mopti Nov 1970
- R. Niger
- GUINEA
- Conakry
- R. Niger
- Kano Feb 1971
- Religious ceremony May 1971
- GHANA
- BENIN
- TOGO
- NIGERIA
- IVORY COAST
- Sept 1970
- Abidjan Oct 1970
- Accra Nov 1970
- Lagos Dec 1970
- CAMEROON
- Douala
- Dec 1970

Legend:
- – – – Stage 1 Coastal diffusion (Sep–Dec 1970) disease carried by fishermen
- ——— Stage 2 Inland penetration (Sep 1970–Feb 1971) carried by merchants and traders
- ● Stage 3 Radial diffusion (Oct 1970–Dec 1971) from urban centres
- – – – Stage 4 Other factors

0   500 km

Study of the spread or diffusion of cholera

In 1961, the El Tor strain of Cholera flared up in the Celebes Island group in S.E. Asia, and spread with amazing speed throughout South and East Asia, reaching India in 1964, and Southern Russia in 1970.

Students returning from Moscow stopped in the Russian Crimea, contracted cholera, and carried the vibrio back to Guinea in West Africa, thereby re-introducing cholera into Africa after an absence of 75 years. From Guinea, the progress or **diffusion** of cholera throughout West Africa has been carefully recorded by Medical Geographers. See Fig. 4.7. This map illustrates the main methods of diffusion.

1. Coastal diffusion from Guinea to the Cameroons by migrating fisherman, who visited a number of lagoons, and infected villages and towns.
2. Inland penetration along roads and rivers by merchants and traders moving inland from such cities as Lagos, Abidjan and Accra.
3. Radial diffusion from urban centres such as Kano and Lagos. Cholera was first recorded in the old south-western sector of Ibadan, where there are inadequate water supplies and poor sanitation. From here, cholera progressively hit the surrounding suburbs and villages.

4. Where large groups of people congregated in 1970 and 1971, the disease spread to new victims. For example, in Chad, 20 000 people assembled for a religious ceremony, and on returning home the vibrio was spread to Niger and Northern Cameroon. Mourners at a funeral in Mali carried the disease back to Senegal, and nomadic herders introduced the disease northwards towards the Sahel.

In conclusion, cholera cannot thrive where water is treated and where environmental sanitation and standards of hygiene can be controlled. In many areas of West Africa these conditions do not exist and so although cholera has largely now died out, there always remains a high probability of a future outbreak.

8. With reference to Fig. 4.7 which shows the spread of cholera in West Africa, briefly describe the paths taken. Suggest the kind of factors which might have encouraged the spread of such an outbreak. What makes such an epidemic difficult to control?

What's dirty, wet and dangerous?

The World Health Organisation estimates that 80% of all sickness and disease can be attributed to inadequate water and sanitation. Such diseases cause an estimated 25 million deaths each year. One child in seven in the developing world dies before his or her fifth birthday. Most of these deaths could have been prevented.

In the case studies which follow, the role played by water is central to the cause and to the eventual solution of the 'waterborne' diseases.

Malaria

According to the W.H.O., malaria is one of the world's most widespread, devastating diseases. (See Fig. 4.8). More than half of the world's population lives in endemic areas, and an estimated 8 to 9 million people die principally from the disease every year. Malaria is known as the 'King of Diseases'.

The symptoms of malaria include high temperatures, sweating and recurrent fever, enlargement of the spleen, lethargy and laziness, and may result in a coma, then death. Malnourished children are very susceptible.

Fig. 4.9 shows the main features of the 'Malarial Cycle.' The female anopheles mosquito carries the malarial parasite or plasmodium. If such a mosquito bites an infected person in order to have 'a blood meal', the parasite enters the mosquito. When that mosquito bites another healthy human, the parasite passes back into the human bloodstream.

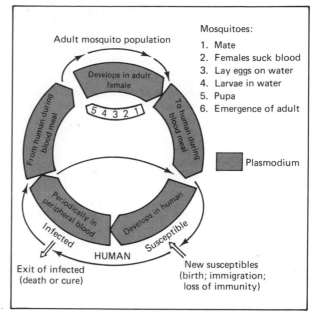

4.9 The malaria cycle

Environmental conditions favouring malaria
The mosquito requires temperatures in excess of 16°C, and a stagnant water surface in order to breed. This water surface can be a lake, an old bomb crater, (as in Vietnam) a tank well, (as in India) irrigation channels and padi fields, or even the earthenware water storage pots used by villagers throughout Tropical Africa and Asia.

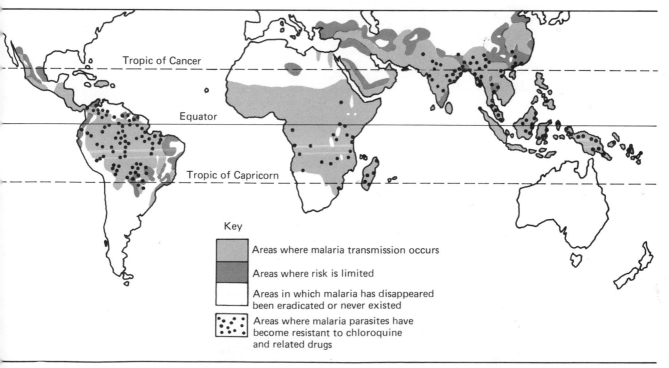

In order to tackle Malaria, the cycle must be broken, either by:

1. eradicating the malarial carrying mosquitoes i.e. the vector, or
2. attacking the parasite, the plasmodium, either in humans or in the mosquito.

The W.H.O. is particularly active with malarial research and control in South East Asia, India, Burma, Mayalsia, Brazil and Papua New Guinea.

1. Malarial eradication by attacking the anopheles mosquito

Method	Problems
Drainage of the breeding grounds	Very expensive, requires incredible manpower, (which is available), and is often impractical as mosquito larvae can hatch in puddles or tin cans
Spray a film of oil on water surfaces, to suffocate the larvae	Very expensive, and wasteful. Impossible to cover all surfaces and pollutes water
Use of insecticides such as D.D.T.	Highly pollutive to all ecosystem, as well as very expensive. Again difficult to spray all habitats. Mosquito resistance becoming common
New pesticides, e.g. Malathion	Again expensive, pollutive and likely resistance factor among mosquito population soon
Larvae parasitic diseases introduced	Very modern development. Good for small areas. Expensive, and may upset whole ecosystem
Genetic Engineering, by introducing sterile males and laboratory bred mercenary mosquitoes	Still in research stage, likely to be expensive and there may be public concern with genetic engineering
Public education, through local health campaigns	Involves organizational skills. Likely to yield high dividends when combined with the above

2. Malarial eradication by attacking the parasite (plasmodium)

Method	Problems
Destroy the plasmodium in the mosquito	Kill the mosquito. See above
Traditional cure. Use of quinine, to kill plasmodium in human host	Increasing, plasmodium resistance to quinine
New synthetic vaccines such as Atabrin	Substitute is expensive and has unpleasant side effects
Vaccines to stop mosquitoes picking up parasites in bloodmeal	Research still needed. A single, long lasting vaccine innoculation is still 10 years away

4.10 Control methods

Control

Governments in several countries have switched money from malaria programmes to other projects as their budgets come under pressure. In India, malaria was almost eradicated in the mid 1960s. However, a combination of events meant that the disease re-established itself. These events included the 1965 Indo-Pakistan War; the closure of the Suez Canal, which delayed the arrival of D.D.T. from the U.S.A.; the oil crisis, which pushed the price of insecticides up too high so that imports ceased; and finally the development by mosquitos of resistance to D.D.T.

The W.H.O. has now abandoned hope of eradicating malaria. Now the emphasis is on control. Strong hopes are pinned on new drugs, vaccines and novel vector control methods. See Fig. 4.10.

Last year 1.7 million trips were made by British people to third world countries, most of which are malarious. About half of these were holiday makers who often were given no warning of the dangers they faced.

In 1985, 2200 people returning to Britain from all parts of the world developed malaria and five died. This puts the risk of travellers to these countries getting malaria at one in about 800 trips.

Case study: Onchocerciasis in West Africa

Onchocerciasis (river blindness) has been described as the most important single factor which retards economic growth in West Africa. The cause of the disease is a parasitic worm, which develops into adult worms in the human body. Whilst in the host, micro filariae from the female worm migrate through the human system and frequently lodge in the eye, or form cyst-like swellings clearly visible under the skin. The symptoms include weight loss, large nodules causing intense itching, urinary tract infection, possible impotence, impaired vision and eventual blindness. The disease is endemic in West Africa. In 1974, prior to a Control Programme, 10% of the population was infected with oncho, although in a number of river valleys the infection rate was often as high as 80%, with up to 15% of the population blind. Several of the tributary valleys of the River Volta had been abandoned by the people. Repeated infections are necessary for severe results, and the disease may take 15 years to fully develop. In 1980 the W.H.O. estimated that there were over 1 million sufferers in West Africa alone, with about 10% blind and another 30% with poor eyesight.

The vector responsible for the transmission of the disease is the female blackfly of the simulium species. In its life span of three weeks, it requires several blood meals. This tiny fly acquires the micro filariae from an infected human, and at a later stage during another blood meal, the micro-filariae larvae will be passed out, infecting another person. Inside the host, the larvae develop into adult male and female worms and breed.

The pattern of the disease is linked to the breeding and feeding requirements of the fly. Black flies need swiftly flowing, oxygenated water, with suitable places for the blackfly larvae to attach. The temperature has to be in excess of 18°C, and the flies have a flight range of 18 km. Most at risk are people living close to breeding sites and within the flight range of the fly.

Oncho and development

Oncho creates unproductive adults. One of the saddest sights is seeing a child leading a number of blind adults by the hand to the fields to work. In time villages and agricultural land close to breeding sites are deserted. As much as 15% of the potentially good farmland in Burkina Faso lies abandoned. This movement away from infected areas produces high population densities elsewhere, resulting in overgrazing and eventual soil erosion.

4.11 Treating a watercourse with larvicide, Burkina Faso

Modern developments can create health problems by helping to form new artificial breeding sites such as in irrigation sluices, waterways and dam outlets. Control of the disease requires finance, co-operation and organized management. Drugs can be used to treat the disease, but they tend to be expensive and cause serious side effects. Established blindness is beyond treatment. Once the human host is infected, treatment is difficult and often of limited use. The real way forward is tackling the insect vector and attacking the larval stages of the flies by adding insecticide to the water in which they breed. Since 1974 the Onchocerciasis Control Programme has been combating the disease in West Africa. The Director of the Control Programme, O.C.P., in October 1985 stated that 90% of the area in the programme was now essentially free form endemic oncho. The cycle of infection had been interrupted, and the land bordering many W. African rivers can now be declared safe for resettlement and farming. The O.C.P. should last 20 years, and the overall aim is to diminish the number of the blackfly pest, so that it no longer transmits the micro filariae from one human victim to another. (See 'A Success Story' p. 44.)

The rivers are sprayed by larvicides, such as abate and chlorphoxin, from the air by helicopter or light aeroplane, on a very regular basis. The cost of the O.C.P. is about $16 million a year, about $1 a year for each inhabitant in the area. Recent research by the W.H.O. indicates that new, more effective larvicides and a possible breakthrough in tackling the adult worms and micro filariae in the human host using chemotherapy, provide encouraging signs for the future. However there is no room for complacency. Much work has yet to be done to ensure that the controlled areas are not re-invaded by the vector and new areas have yet to be cleared.

A success story

Seven countries of West Africa requested the W.H.O. in 1970 to prepare a strategy for a programme to control onchocerciasis – river blindness – in the Volta River Basin area.

These first member countries of what became the Onchocerciasis Control Programme (O.C.P.) were: Benin (formerly Dahomey), Burkina Faso (formerly Upper Volta), Ghana, Ivory Coast, Mali, Niger and Togo.

In 1974, intensive spraying of larvicide against the blackfly really began over an area of 654 000 sq km, including some 14 500 km of river. 1985 is halfway in what was envisaged as a 20-year programme.

In 90 per cent of that area, transmission of the disease is considered by the W.H.O. to be 'under control.' Among the 16 million people living in the area, more than 3 million are children born since the programme began who are free of the disease and are no longer at risk of losing their sight through river blindness.

Four new countries will join the programme in 1986: Guinea, Guinea-Bissau, Senegal, and Sierra Leone. The programme area will then cover 1 300 000 sq km – virtually all the natural habitat in West Africa of the blackfly species which transmits the blinding form of onchocerciasis.

9. Examine Fig. 4.8. Describe and explain the distribution of malaria referring to both human and physical factors.

10. Study Fig. 4.9 (Malarial Cycle). Describe this cycle, and explain how it can be broken.

11. Design your own diagram, similar to Fig. 4.9, showing the Onchocerciasis cycle. Describe the environmental conditions which favour the spread of oncho.

12. Describe the work of the O.C.P., commenting on the success or otherwise, at the half way stage of the 20 year programme.

Case study: Schistosomiasis (Bilharzia)

Around 90% of the population of developing countries live in areas where Schistosomiasis is endemic and the W.H.O. estimate that some 200 million people are currently infected. The cause is the schistosome worm, which is exchanged backwards and forwards between humans and a certain freshwater snail (see Fig. 4.13). This exchange takes place in slow moving shallow water which, in conditions of poor hygiene, often serves as sewer, bath and well. Ironically, many programmes of irrigation and the creation of new waterways, such

4.12 Child leading an adult blinded by Onchocerciasis

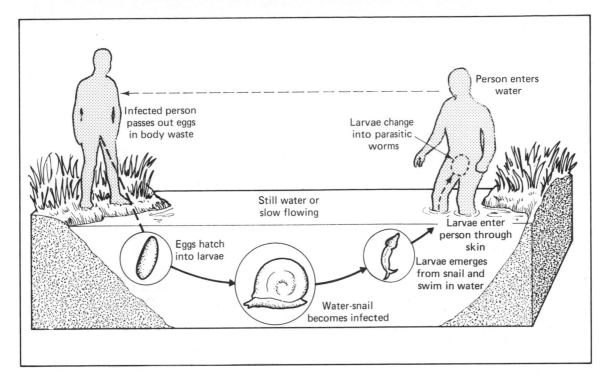

4.13 Cycle of transmission: schistosomiasis

as Lake Nasser in Egypt, have exacerbated the problem.

Control methods include chemotherapy to kill the worm in the human host, but this and other drug treatments often have unpleasant side effects. Alternatively, molluscicides can be introduced to kill the snails, or snail eating fish can be used. Prevention is a better approach. The Chinese have had considerable success with massive environmental and public health education programmes. There is a need to separate the three functions for water use. Improved sanitation, pure drinking water from an unpolluted source and public awareness of the dangers of swimming or washing in infected waters are all essential.

However successful control projects are, it is important that they be maintained. In the Sudan, several villages were free from Bilharzia in 1977 following 5 years of chemotherapy and snail control. In 1986, as a result of re-infection, the disease was again endemic. A final point that should be included in any consideration of this and other diseases is the importance of political stability. Political unrest in a country will obviously make the work of controlling or eradicating disease very difficult. However, given time, resources, international cooperation and relatively stable conditions, most of the above diseases can be brought under some sort of control.

13. Discuss the role of water in the distribution of Bilharzia, and explain how the disease is transmitted.

14. Explain the importance of international co-operation in the fight against disease.

Contrasting disease patterns

So far we have mainly looked at infectious and diet related diseases in the poorer lands of the world. The pattern of death in the developed world is different. (See Fig. 4.14, showing death statistics in Scotland 1985.) The four major causes of death in a developed country such as Scotland are all non-infectious, and can be linked to environmental and 'lifestyle' factors. Here, the environment is essentially dominated by urban living, an industrialized landscape, all within a society full of the 'pressures of daily life'. Deaths due to infectious diseases are rare in a developed society.

Unlike some of the diseases studied above, there are few 'cures' for these. Preventative measures need to be taken to alter environmental conditions and educate the population towards a change in lifestyles. Attitudinal changes take a long time to work. Several of the so called 'rich world' diseases are self-inflicted, with clear medically proved links to excessive drinking, imbalanced diet and eating habits, and smoking.

45

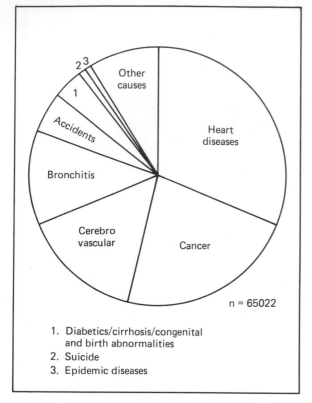

4.14 Pattern of death in Scotland – 1985

1. Diabetics/cirrhosis/congenital and birth abnormalities
2. Suicide
3. Epidemic diseases

A recent report (1985) by the Health Education Council (H.E.C.) stated that smoking in England and Wales directly caused the early death of some 77 000 people in 1984. A further 110 000 people were admitted to hospitals with smoking related diseases, such as heart disease, lung cancer, bronchitis and emphysema. Added to this human suffering, is the cost to the Nation and to the Health Service of some £111 million. The latest Government statistics indicate that 14% of all deaths are related, if not, due to smoking. The H.E.C. in their report note that smoking rates amongst the adult population are falling, with only 30% now smoking.

Within Britain, there are clearly defined patterns. Smoking and associated illnesses are far more common in the north and north-west, with over 19% of all deaths linked to smoking, whilst in the south in the Oxford area the figure is 10%. The geographical differences can also be noted with cancers. (See Fig. 4.15.)

The H.E.C. is also concerned about the problems resulting from alcohol (see Fig. 4.16). Alcoholism is the fourth largest cause of death in France, directly responsible for the deaths of some 20 000 people. Alcoholics cost the country nearly

Glasgow the world's worst cancer city

The spread of cancer throughout Scotland, with Glasgow the world's worst city for lung cancer in men, is charted in a major study of the disease published yesterday.

The Atlas of Cancer in Scotland, 1975–1980, is an illustrated breakdown of the incidence and geographical distribution of the disease in its many forms, which attempts to uncover the factors which influence its course.

Most strikingly Scotland is shown to have one of the worst rates in the world of lung cancer, the deadliest of them all, among men with an incidence of 91.4 per 100 000, and Glasgow emerges as the outright worst, at 130.6 per thousand.

What this means, the compilers of the atlas explained yesterday, is that there will be one new case for every 500 males in the city each year. Put another way, each man or boy has a one-in-six chance of contracting the disease. Few survive.

Female rates are also high – although breast cancer is still the most prevalent form of the disease in women – and the atlas is seen as vindicating the Glasgow 2000 campaign to make the city non-smoking by the end of the century.

Other cancers on the increase are also attributed, at least in part, to smoking, with heavy drinking and diet the other principal behavioural factors.

It was prepared by the World Health Organization's International Agency for Research on Cancer, using data supplied by the regional cancer registries of Scotland.

Scottish Secretary Mr George Younger, commenting on the survey in a Commons written reply last night, said: 'Those forms of cancer most prevalent in Scotland seem to be associated with tobacco, spirits, and diets with an excess of fat and a deficiency of fresh vegetables and other fibre.'

Measures already the subject of Government action in the health education field – on smoking, drinking, and diet – would, if heeded by the public, lead to a significant reduction in cancer rates.

'Government funding of research into the causes, prevention management, and cure of cancer will continue at its present high level, and I would expect the research needs identified in the atlas to form the basis of new and productive research in the years ahead.'

4.15 Article from *The Glasgow Herald*, 29.11.85

The liver is like a car with only one gear – it can only work at one rate. The liver can only burn up one standard drink in an hour. If it has to deal with too much alcohol over a number of years, it suffers damage.

Excessive drinking can cause:
■ hepatitis (inflammation of the liver) and cirrhosis (permanent scarring of the liver) ■ stomach disorders (gastritis, bleeding and ulcers) ■ cancer of the mouth, throat and gullet ■ brain damage ■ sexual difficulties ■ depression and other psychiatric disorders ■ high blood pressure ■ muscle disease ■ problems with the nervous system (especially nerve pains in the legs and arms) ■ vitamin deficiency ■ It can also add to the problems of people with diabetes.

4.16 Alcohol: the long term effects

£900 million when absenteeism from work and hospitalization costs are totalled.

A healthy population is thus less costly to a Government than an unhealthy one, and Government backed groups such as the Health Education Council and the Scottish Health Education Group actively promote the 're-education' of the British people.

Medical opinion seems to agree that diets should move towards low cholesterol, low salt and high fibre intake. More recently the whole question of food additives has been raised, and it is becoming more acceptable and fashionable to be vegetarian, or follow health food programmes. More and more people are now participating actively in physical pursuits such as squash, jogging and even marathon running. However we still live in a world of fast or 'junk' foods. Again attitudinal changes take a long time to alter the habits of a nation.

Urban living with its combination of high stress and generally low physical activity is a prime cause of cerebral strokes and heart failure. No longer is this solely a developed world problem. For example the Masai herdsmen of East Africa are virtually immune to heart diseases, as long as they stay in the countryside. Once they move to the city they are prone to develop the so-called **'executive diseases'**, for city life seems to encourage changes in diet and lifestyle. In 1948 in Singapore, when life expectancy was 50 years, the leading causes of death were tuberculosis and other infectious diseases. By 1985, life expectancy was 71 years and cardiovascular disease was the leading cause of death.

A relatively new virus has now appeared in the developed world. Aids (Acquired Immune Deficiency Syndrome), believed to have originated in Africa, is now sending shock waves around the world. The virus affects the body's 'immunity to infection'. The virus, for which there is no cure yet, is transmitted from a carrier to another human in blood and other body fluids. For example, it may be transmitted to a patient receiving a transfusion of blood donated by a carrier, to someone being injected with a needle that has been used with a carrier and not sterilised, or to someone having sexual intercourse with a carrier.

Alternative models of health care

The W.H.O.'s goal for the year 2000 is . . . 'Health for all.' They define health as 'a state of complete physical, mental and social well being', and not merely the absence of disease or infirmity. Health care provision varies greatly between the developed and developing world (see Fig. 4.17) as well as within developing countries. Urban areas have a disproportionate number of doctors, nurses, and modern hospitals, often leaving the majority of the population in rural communities lacking in health schemes and cover. Trained medical workers are often disinclined to work in the countryside. However, as Fig. 4.19 shows, such problems can be overcome. Such a model of health care provision may indeed be the only realistic plan for improved health services for the whole population of a developing country.

The Medical Aide (or **'Barefoot Doctor'**) fulfills a local community need for ready access to treatment, preventative services and health education. These trained Aides are locally known, trusted and available. If more advanced treatment is necessary, the patient can then be passed on to the doctor, who can concentrate on such matters without being burdened by the heavy day to day workload of common ailments.

	Population per hospital bed	Population per physician
NIGERIA	1251	9591
BRAZIL	245	1632
MEXICO	863	2136
USSR	80	267
USA	177	549
SCOTLAND	88	551
INDIA	1265	2545
ETHIOPIA	2787	72 582

4.17 Contrasts in health care

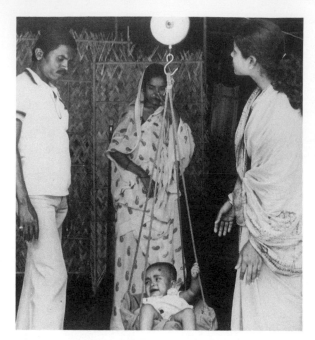

4.18 Monitoring nutrition to detect vitamin A deficiency and prevent blindness

The Nicaraguan Government in 1980 took stock of an appalling health problem – infant mortality reaching 30%; endemic tuberculosois and malaria (40% of the population had malaria), 70% of children were malnourished. Primary Health Care was identified as a priority area, and within 4 years some 500 new health centres had been opened in rural areas. Infant mortality rates had been reduced to 9% and massive vaccination campaigns eradicated polio. Malaria was only to be found in 3% of rural dwellers, and a new medical school was opened. Real progress was being made. Unfortunately in recent years the guerilla war and economic crisis have resulted in a virtual collapse of many of the health care schemes.

Massive international action can supplement such community programmes. Smallpox, now eradicated worldwide, was subject to 12 years of concentrated action, at a cost of some $300 million. The U.N.O. estimate that such action has resulted in yearly savings of $1000 million.

In the developed world, Governments can choose their priorities for economic and social development, with education, health, defence, social services, law and order, housing and others, all challenging for a larger share of the 'economic pie'. Health provision in Britain for 1986/87 will cost in excess of £21 670 million. That is approximately £400 for every man, woman and child in the country.

Fig. 4.20 shows a possible model for health care provision within a developed country. The environment contains many health hazards, but a government can take steps to protect its people from birth throughout life. Health care provision is not cheap, but it is nevertheless much cheaper to prevent diseases than to cure them.

The future?

Disease is a hindrance to progress, and results in extreme human suffering. As geographers, we have studied the link between disease and the physical and social environments.

For a country to develop, all resources should be used to their full potential. The most important resource any country has is its people. Sick people become a liability, and have to be cared for and supported by the rest of that society.

So where is the hope for the future? In the developing world, there are countless examples of positive measures being taken . . . a swamp being drained; a new sewer being laid; health clinics opened and so on. Whether this is inspired and financed by the local government, or by world agencies such as the World Health Organisation, or supported by the charity groups, such as Band Aid, or Oxfam, the end result can only be to the benefit of all.

15. The term 'executive disease' was used in the text. Why should such a description be used with reference to cerebral strokes?

16. 'Disease reflects the development of a society.' Explain this statement with reference to both the developed and the developing world. Mention specific diseases and their causes.

17. What steps can a government take to ensure the continuing health of its people? Give specific details of examples known to you.

18. Study Figs. 4.19 and 4.20.
   a) Briefly describe the main features of each model.
   b) Explain why Fig. 4.20 is not the model that can be, or should be, followed in a developing country.

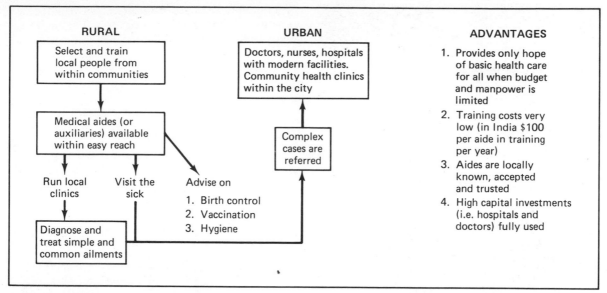

4.19 Model for health care provision in developing countries

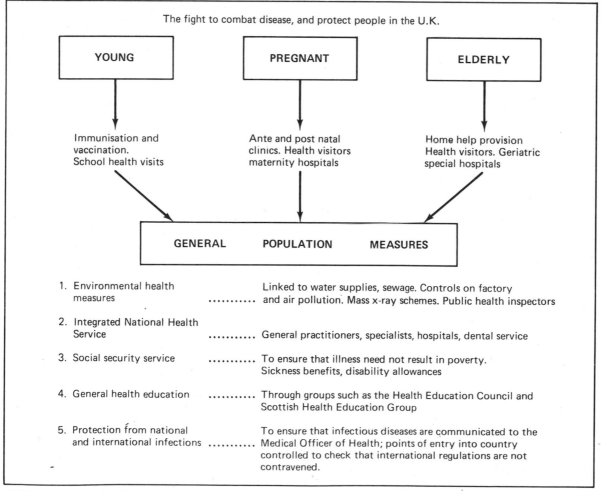

4.20 Model for health care provision in developed countries

5

Urbanization

Urbanization refers to the increasing percentage of a country's population who live in cities and to the various economic and social causes and effects of this. The dramatic increase in a country's urban population is partly accounted for by the natural growth in the urban population discussed in Chapter 2 and partly by the influx of migrants who migrate to live in towns and cities. (Recent studies have shown that 50% of Bogota's population and 48% of Lima's are not locally born.)

In 1985 just over 40% of the world's total population lived in urban areas leaving the majority of the world's population still living as rural dwellers (Fig. 5.1). However, this statistic hides the very important point that the increase in urbanization over the years has been very great and in some countries is so rapid or is at such a high percentage that severe problems have arisen. Indeed, urbanization is proceeding at such a rate that by the year 2005 it is estimated that for the first time in human history the majority of the world's population will be urban dwellers. Fig. 5.2 shows the rates of urbanization in several countries.

1. Use the information in Fig. 5.1 to comment for developed and developing countries on:
   (a) the % urban and rural figures;
   (b) the average rates of annual urban increase;
   (c) the average rates of annual rural increase.

2. Describe the patterns shown in Fig. 5.2.

3. What evidence is there from Figs. 5.1 and 5.2 that urbanization is generally considered to be more of a 'third world problem' than that of the richer, developed world?

As we shall find out, it would be wrong to assume that the process and resultant problems of urbanization are confined solely to the rapidly and more recently expanding cities of the third world. Long-established, highly urbanized societies in the developed world also have their own particular

	WORLD	AFRICA	LATIN AMERICA	NORTH AMERICA	EAST ASIA	SOUTH ASIA	EUROPE	OCEANIA	U.S.S.R.
% URBAN									
1950	29.4	14.8	41.1	63.9	17.8	16.1	55.9	61.3	39.3
1980	39.9	28.7	65.3	73.8	28.0	25.4	71.1	71.6	63.2
2000	48.2	42.2	76.6	78.0	34.2	36.8	79.0	73.1	74.3
2025	62.5	58.3	84.2	85.8	51.2	55.3	85.9	78.4	83.4
AVERAGE RATE OF ANNUAL INCREASE									
URBAN									
1955	3.1	4.3	4.6	2.7	4.3	3.3	1.6	3.1	3.9
1980	2.6	5.3	3.6	1.1	2.1	4.1	1.1	1.6	2.0
2000	2.5	4.7	2.4	1.2	2.5	3.6	0.7	1.5	1.4
2025	1.9	3.1	1.5	0.8	1.8	2.2	0.3	1.2	0.9
AVERAGE RATE OF ANNUAL INCREASE									
RURAL									
1955	1.3	1.7	1.3	0.0	1.5	1.7	−0.2	0.9	0.1
1980	1.3	2.1	0.3	1.1	1.2	1.7	−1.2	1.7	−0.7
2000	0.6	1.9	0.1	−0.6	0.4	0.6	−1.3	0.7	−1.0
2025	−0.5	0.5	−0.4	−1.2	−1.0	−0.7	−1.6	−0.2	−1.2

5.1 Percentage urban/rural and rates of increase − 1950–2020

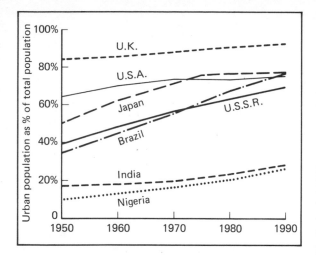

5.2 Growth of urban population

problems and these will be studied at the end of the chapter.

Millionaire and super cities

Cities which have become highly urbanized and which now exceed a population of one million are known as millionaire cities. In 1950 there were 59 millionaire cities in the world and only 7 urban centres/**metropolitan areas** with populations exceeding 5 million making them super cities (Fig. 5.3). Today there are over 180 millionaire cities and 34 super cities and such has been the rate of urbanization that many cities are growing to become super cities, with an estimated 93 likely to have populations in excess of 5 million by the year 2025 (Fig. 5.3).

Primate cities

In some countries, for example, Mexico, Chile, Egypt, Venezuela and Indonesia, urbanization has been highly concentrated in one particular millionaire or super city. Such a city, often the capital, is usually many times larger than the next largest city and is where most of the economic growth and urban problems exist. It is known as a primate city.

4. Using Fig. 5.3 draw up a list of the largest cities in the world in 1950, 1985 and 2025.

5. In which continents were most of the millionaire and super cities in 1950 and 1985?

6. Between which latitudes and in which continents are most of the millionaire and super cities expected to be found by 2025? What pattern appears to be emerging?

7. Use an atlas to help you name the 5 primate cities mentioned in the text above.

Why cities grow – push and pull factors

Fig. 5.2 showed us that, once started, the rate of urbanization in the developed countries in the 19th and early 20th centuries increased dramatically before levelling off. Much of the attraction of cities was related to rapid industrialization and the need for labour in factories, mills, shipyards and mines. In the third world today, cities still act as magnets 'pulling' people away from the countryside. Recent figures estimate that in Sao Paulo up to 500 000 migrants per year are being attracted to the city. However, what contributes as much to urbanization in the third world is the lack of development in the rural areas which 'pushes' people away from the rural countryside. These 'push' and 'pull' factors that contribute to urbanization can be broadly divided into four groups (i) social factors (ii) economic factors (iii) political factors and (iv) physical factors. While such a 'push' and 'pull' view of migration has been criticised as being an over-simplification of the very complex reasons for migration it does, none-the-less, serve to illustrate some of the major causes and decisions which force rural dwellers to move to urban areas and add to the process and problems of urbanization.

Like ants from the cracks

When all else fails in overcrowded Java, the island where two-thirds of Indonesians live, a jobless villager heads for Jakarta. In the nation's capital he can pedal a pedicab, hawk food from a push cart or, if he sinks right to the bottom, join the rag-pickers who scavenge cigarette butts. A succession of military governors of Jakarta has fought to make the villagers stay out. One, in 1971, decreed Jakarta a 'closed city' in an attempt to end what he said was an annual flood of 200 000 Javanese peasants.

The governors have lost their 15-year battle. Despite identity cards, police sweeps and razed shantytowns, along with periodic outlawing of pedicabs and street vendors, yearly migration from the villages never fell below 80 000. Now it is back up to over 250 000. With Indonesia's oil-dependent economy faltering, it could go higher. Jakarta, whose population rose from 1.7 m to 5 m in 1950–70, now officially has 7.5 m people; the real figure is probably closer to 9 m. Like ants from the cracks, they keep coming.

The Economist, Feb 1 1986

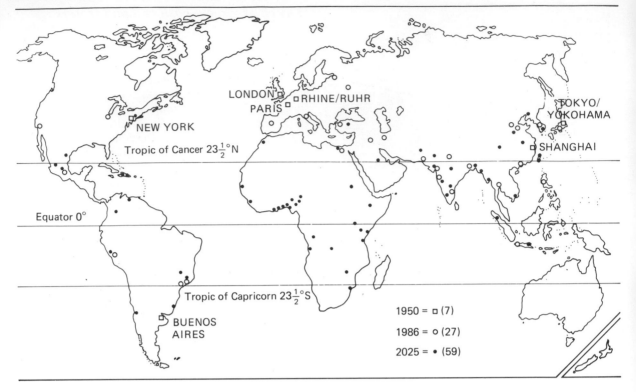

5.3 Super cities – 1950, 1986 and projected 2025

Social factors

In many third world countries there is considerable pressure on the rural land through overpopulation. This results, in part, from high birth rates which can be caused directly by religious objections to the use of family planning methods and to the social status attached to and the need for large families to carry out the work in rural areas. One consequence of these high birth rates is that many people are added to the numbers that have to be supported by the land and that people leave for urban areas to relieve pressure on families and on the land. In India an important social custom resulting in rural migration is the movement of a bride to her husband's home. However, of greater importance in India has been the escape from caste restrictions brought about by a move to cities from the countryside.

Economic factors

Farming in rural areas can be extremely hard with long working hours and little financial return. The resultant poverty and deprivation combined with a shortage of land through sub-division, a reduction in jobs through mechanisation and lack of facilities such as hospitals and schools have all been very powerful motives for movement to urban centres. On the 'pull' side, the prospects of a factory job in the city which may bring in wages many times that possible through farm work has been an important incentive to migration. So also are the perceptions of better housing, better services, more entertainment, more reliable sources of food and the overall expectation of a higher quality of life offered by the urban areas.

Political factors

Civil wars and religious persecution throughout many countries and areas (India, Bangladesh, Pakistan, Nigeria, Afghanistan, Uganda, the Middle East and Central America) have created many millions of **refugees** and forced these people to move to new areas and new countries. On a smaller scale, indigenous peoples such as in the Amazon have been displaced as a result of mineral and agricultural developments. Generally, such landless people have looked to the urban areas for the opportunity of employment, housing and a new future. It has also been suggested that political and religious activities can be carried on more safely and more effectively in large urban centres and this too can contribute to the 'drift' to the cities.

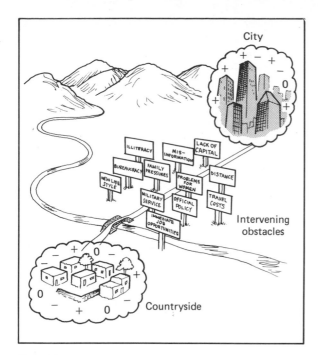

5.4 Migration model

Physical factors

Natural disasters such as flooding (Bangladesh), hurricanes (Caribbean), mud avalanches (Peru) and severe, prolonged drought (N.E. Brazil and the Sahel countries of Africa) with their resultant destruction of villages, loss of crops and livelihood, crop failure and starvation have forced many rural villagers off the land and into urban towns and cities. The degradation of farmland through poor farming techniques and mass deforestation has also led to soils being rendered useless for farming and this has forced rural peasants to leave the land.

The problems involved in migration to urban areas are shown in Fig. 5.4.

8. Which age group and sex of the rural population are most likely to migrate to the city and why?

9. What problems are created in the rural villages with this 'drift' and, in some cases, 'rush' to the city?

10. List some of the obstacles which have to be overcome if the migrant is to reach the city.

Problems of urbanization

It is the increasing size of city populations generally and in millionaire and super cities specifically that has brought about many of the problems found in them today. In many such third world cities it has created slums and **shanty towns**, compounded social inequalities and created a demand for basic facilities such as clean water, employment, education, medical care and sanitation which is almost impossible to meet.

While the main problems caused by rapid urbanization are most clearly seen in the large urban centres of the third world, the effects of urbanization can be far-reaching. This tremendous concentration of people and industry can lead to serious problems in 'downstream' rural areas. The River Bogota which runs through the Colombian capital is contaminated by effluents from industry, sewage and run-off from the city's 5 million inhabitants. At Tocaima, 120 km downstream the river was reported in 1980 to be black and smelling of sewage and chemicals and to be totally unfit for drinking or cooking. The La Paz river, which passes through Bolivia's capital, has become so polluted that horticultural production has been stopped downstream.

It is in the shanty towns, found in most of the rapidly expanding third world cities, that many of the problems of urbanization can be most vividly seen. A shanty town is an area of very poor quality housing into which many of the rural migrants first move and live on coming to the city. Shanty towns vary greatly in their appearance and in facilities, but can be broadly divided into two main groups:
(i) **inner city slums** – usually downgraded former residential blocks which belonged to low and middle income groups. While many tend to have some basic facilities they have become severely overcrowded causing considerable pressure and

5.5 Poor urban conditions, Lagos, Nigeria

City (Country)	Total pop. (millions)	Approximate shanty town pop. %
BOGOTA (Colombia)	5.0	60%
BOMBAY (India)	6.0	42%
CARACAS (Venezuela)	3.5	42%
HYDERABAD (India)	2.6	40%
IBADAN (Nigeria)	1.2	75%
JAKARTA (Indonesia)	6.5	26%
KARACHI (Pakistan)	5.5	23%
KINSHASA (Zaire).	2.5	55%
LIMA (Peru)	3.6	43%
MADRAS (India)	4.4	20%
MANILA (Philippines)	5.9	35%
RIO DE JANIERO (Brazil)	5.1	30%
SEOUL (S. Korea)	8.4	22%

5.6 Selected shanty town populations – 1985

So great are the problems found in some shanty towns and so large are some of the shanty town populations (Fig. 5.6) that the term 'miseropolis' has been given to many third world urban centres such as Calcutta, Lagos, Lima, Caracas and Manila.

Shanty towns go by a variety of names depending upon the part of the world or city they are found in:
bustees, cheris, jhuggies (India, Pakistan, Bangladesh)
barriadas (Lima, Peru)
barong-barongs (Philippines)
favelas (Brazil)
villas miserias, ranchos (Venezuela)
jacales, colonias proletarias (Mexico)
gecekundu (Ankara, Turkey)
callampas (Chile)
bidonvilles (N. Africa).

breakdown of services. Some have developed into illegal or semi-legal 'squatter' settlements since so few migrants can afford to pay rents for the property. A recent estimate calculated that only 12% of Manila's population could afford to buy or rent a legal house or flat on the open market. It is, however, into many of these inner city slums that many migrants in places like South America proceed on first moving to the city before then moving to more peripheral areas.

(ii) **peripheral slums** – faced with no legal, affordable shelter, many migrants to the city frequently build 'spontaneous', 'squatter' settlements illegally on the periphery of the city and, to a much lesser extent, near the inner city. Such shanty towns consist of simple one-roomed shacks made from cardboard, sacking and corrugated iron sheeting with few amenities such as running water, toilets, sewerage and power.

The growth of such shanty towns is nowhere seen better than in Nouakchott (Mauritania) where much of the city's 45 fold increase in population between 1965 and 1985 has been housed in such illegal, 'spontaneous' settlements. Basic service provision is so poor that over 70% of the city's population have no access to water and it frequently has to be bought from water merchants, with no guarantee of quality, at up to 100 times the cost of piped water.

In some cities, however, where such shanty towns have been in existence for many years, some attempts have been made through 'self-help' schemes and other government initiatives, to improve the basic houses with modern building materials and to improve the **infrastructure** by providing public water pumps.

11. What diseases are most likely to develop and spread under the conditions found in the poorer shanty towns?

Sites and locations of shanty towns

Many of the 'spontaneous' shanty towns tend to develop on sites that are illegal and generally unwanted or unsuitable for traditional settlements – hilly areas (Lima, Caracas, Rio de Janiero), rubbish tips (Salvador, Lagos), open derelict land (Calcutta), tidal inudation (Bangkok, Yaounde) or even in swamps (San Juan, Guayaquil, Monrovia, Port Moresby). In Mexico City over 1.5 million people live on the drained bed of Texcoco. This land is subject to dust storms in the dry season and becomes a bog when it rains.

However, just as these 'spontaneous settlements' can vary greatly in site and appearance, they can also vary in their location within a city. Fig. 5.7 gives some idea of where shanty towns might be found and why they are located there.

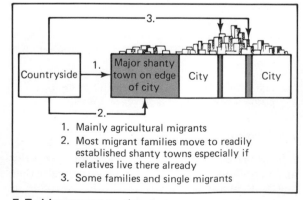

5.7 Movement to shanty towns

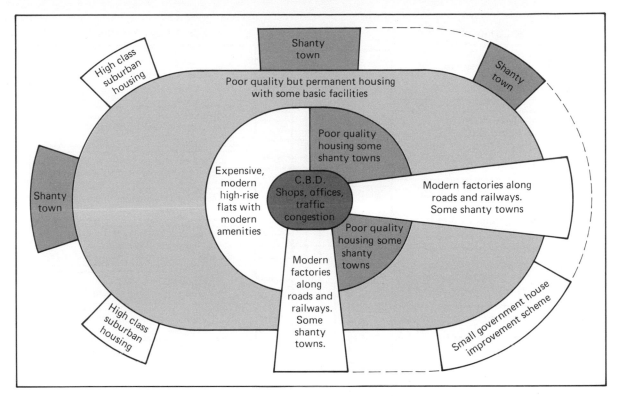

5.8 Model of a third world city

Model of a third world city

Although all cities are unique in their location, layout and the problems they face it is possible to devise a general model which can be applied to cities in the third world (Fig. 5.8).

12. Outline the differences in urban layout between the model for a third world city (Fig. 5.8) and models for a city in the developed world.

Shanty town solutions

The size of the problem facing city authorities with shanty towns is immense. It is best illustrated with some facts for various cities from around the third world:

In Lagos half of the population is under 15 years of age. The figure is 70% in Nairobi.

In Calcutta, 80% of bustee huts are shared by 5 families.

Under 50% of the houses in Rio de Janiero are linked to the public sewers.

Bombay's population in 1985 was over 9 million. U.N. estimates suggest it will double by 2000AD.

Sao Paulo's 1300 different bus routes have to cope with 7 million passengers/day at an average speed of 3 km/hour.

In Jakarta in the late 1970s, total money allocated for all municpal works amounted to £3.50 per head of population.

Migrants arrive in Rio de Janiero at the rate of about 5000 every week. It is estimated that this total migration in all third world countries is as high as 75 000 people every day.

70% of Sao Paulo's houses have no drains.

In Madras only 28% of the total population is classified as having a job.

Each year 80 000 people move to Caracas from the countryside.

In Sierra Leone, only 5% of the households have access to flush toilets.

What makes the problems of the shanty towns seem even more difficult to solve is the fact that in attempting to solve some of the problems many others are created (Fig. 5.9).

Long term and short term

Many third world countries, in looking at the developed world, have seen their 19th and 20th century urbanization as a means through which economic and social development has been achieved and they are prepared to accept any short term problems for what are seen as the prospects of longer term development. However, recent reports have suggested that urbanization in third world

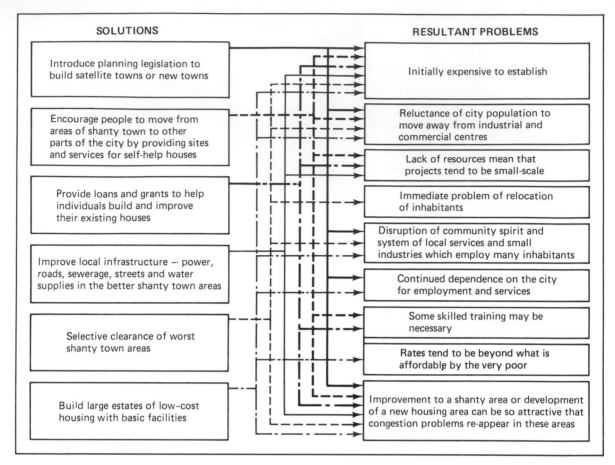

SOLUTIONS	RESULTANT PROBLEMS
Introduce planning legislation to build satellite towns or new towns	Initially expensive to establish
Encourage people to move from areas of shanty town to other parts of the city by providing sites and services for self-help houses	Reluctance of city population to move away from industrial and commercial centres
	Lack of resources mean that projects tend to be small-scale
Provide loans and grants to help individuals build and improve their existing houses	Immediate problem of relocation of inhabitants
	Disruption of community spirit and system of local services and small industries which employ many inhabitants
Improve local infrastructure — power, roads, sewerage, streets and water supplies in the better shanty town areas	Continued dependence on the city for employment and services
	Some skilled training may be necessary
Selective clearance of worst shanty town areas	Rates tend to be beyond what is affordable by the very poor
Build large estates of low-cost housing with basic facilities	Improvement to a shanty area or development of a new housing area can be so attractive that congestion problems re-appear in these areas

5.9 Model for shanty town development

countries may in fact be hindering the achievement of economic and social progress through the costly and seemingly intractable problems it can create, of which shanty towns are an example.

In searching for longer term and lasting solutions to these problems geographers are now considering whether they might not be found by looking towards the rural countryside. In some countries such as Kenya and Zaire, all unemployed youths in the cities are returned to work in the countryside in an attempt to cut down on in-migration to the cities. In Indonesia, all unemployed workers are taken to rehabilitation centres from which they are then sent to work in the countryside. Such schemes have had limited success since many of those returning to the countryside are attracted, at a later date, back to the city. However, by lessening this 'pull' of the cities, through redirection of some investment and development to the more rural areas and smaller urban centres, it is thought that some long-term progress may be made. Such a process of **'decentralisation'** or 'deconcentration' is being attempted in Sao Paulo (see p. 59).

While some hope may lie in implementing such longer term programmes, shorter term schemes have been necessary to cope with the very immediate problems urbanization creates, in particular the shanty towns. In dealing with shanty towns in the short-term, many governments have chosen as an immediate measure to remove the symptom rather than the cause. In Manila, Tripoli, Colombo and Nairobi the shanty towns have been flattened. In Bangkok in 1981, 62 000 shanty town inhabitants were evicted and 150 000 others are threatened with eviction. In Abidjan (Ivory Coast) the mass demolition programme was an attempt to improve housing conditions but its effect was quite the opposite as people simply moved to other areas and established new 'spontaneous' settlements or crowded into existing shanty towns.

As can be seen in the case study of Calcutta (p. 57), **'self-help' schemes** and public works investment aimed at improving shanty towns have had some success. But there, as in many third world cities, the problem still remains as how best to provide legal, affordable 'minimum standard' housing with basic infrastructure and services for the naturally increasing and migrating population.

Some geographers suggest that until lower income groups secure an adequate and stable income, no strategy to improve their environment can ever have any lasting effect. Others suggest that shanty town conditions and other problems brought about by rapid urbanization cannot be expected to improve in nations with poor or bankrupt economies.

13. 'Shanty towns are a reflection of urban growth rather than a symptom of urban decay.' Discuss.

14. 'What is needed are not policies to knock down shanty towns and rehouse a few in concrete boxes. The main aim should be to improve the shanty town'. Discuss the advantages and disadvantages of this proposal.

Calcutta

Calcutta and Howrah make up a twin city of 9.2 million people situated in rural West Bengal on the banks of the Hooghly River 200 km from the Bay of Bengal. It has been widely recognised as one of the world's problem cities and, in many instances, the problems of Calcutta epitomise those of urbanized society in the third world. The city, with its infamous Black Hole, has been described as 'the

1901	1911	1921	1931	1941	1951
1.49	1.72	1.85	2.11	3.58	4.59

1961	1971	1981	% growth 1901–81
5.74	7.03	9.17	615

5.10 The growth of Calcutta's population

world's worst slum'. Although rural to urban migration and natural increase have helped to create some of the city's problems, its physical location is also a major contributory factor.

The dramatic growth of Calcutta can be seen in Fig. 5.10. The city originally developed as a port trading mainly in jute and tea, much of which was grown in the fertile lands of eastern India and what is now Bangladesh. This attracted many workers from the surrounding countryside to work in the many factories such as jute mills, set up along the banks of the river. Although today many of these industries have declined, it is the physical location of Calcutta as a city of size in a predominantly rural area that still makes it a centre of attraction for many rural migrants in West Bengal, Orissa and Bihar states who seek urban employment. Also, the physical situation of the city only a metre or so

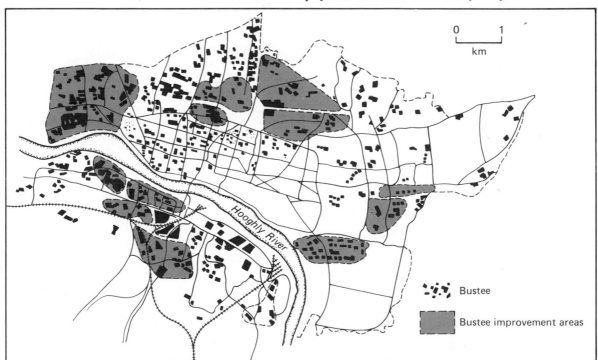

5.11 Land-use in the Calcutta metropolitan area

57

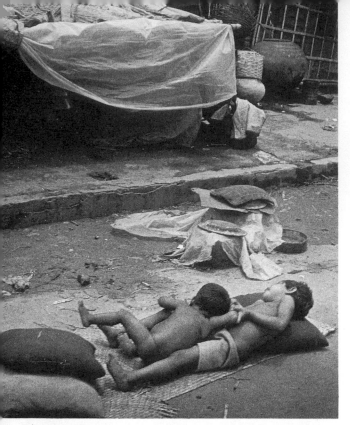

5.12 Living on the street, Calcutta, India

above the flood plain of the river in a flat, humid, swampy area which can suffer some of the worst extremes of a monsoon climate has meant that severe flooding is fairly common, leading to problems of drainage and sewerage.

Today, Calcutta's metropolitan area stretches for over 50 km along the banks of the Hooghly and it is an extremely congested and overcrowded city. The constant influx of rural job seekers together with the natural growth of the city's indigenous population has meant that population density is as high as 30 000 people/km² in some areas – about three times the density of New York. The city's growth has led to a severe housing shortage with nearly one-third of the city's population living in shanty town settlements called 'bustees' (Fig. 5.11).

As in most third world cities, these makeshift slums are constructed of cardboard, corrugated iron, wood and sacking. In the case of Calcutta, many homes are made from dried mud and flood and fall apart during the wet monsoon season. Many of these single-roomed mud shacks were originally intended to house young rural bachelors who moved to the city for part of the year to work and earn money in the mills and factories. They then moved back to their village for sowing and harvest. However, with the shortage of housing

many of these single-roomed shacks have become dwellings for one or more families. Provision of services such as sewerage, water and power in the overcrowded bustees is poor. It is estimated that in the city as a whole 85% of the population have no access to independent bathrooms or to their own piped water supply. Calcutta's drainage system, where it does exist, is over one hundred years old and leaking sewers constantly contaminate drinking water. Rubbish collection, especially in the bustees, is at best irregular, at worst, non-existent. Calcutta's streets become the rubbish dumps with rubbish lying for up to several weeks. It is on these streets that up to half a million of the city's population are estimated to live as street dwellers – the very poorest of the rural poor forced through poverty and unemployment to beg or provide menial, low paid services which earn them only enough money for food and no housing (Fig. 5.12). It is these very visible signs of poverty and destitution that have contributed to Calcutta's image as 'the world's worst city' and which led a group of British and American geographers to comment that they 'had not seen human degradation on a comparable scale in any other city in the world'.

In the 1960s it was obvious that steps had to be taken to try and tackle Calcutta's pressing problems of congested slum housing, poor, inefficient and outdated public services such as water supply and drainage and an overcrowded transport system. As a result, The Calcutta Metropolitan Development Authority (C.M.D.A.) was established in 1970 to implement a 20 year Basic Development Plan for the Calcutta Metropolitan District. In this plan was set out an integrated approach to the problems of housing, water supply, sanitation, transport and development. At the same time the government launched a massive family planning campaign in an attempt to reduce the birth rates and slow population growth throughout the urban centres of India. Clinics were set up in the bustee areas and bustee improvement areas were established which included self-help schemes. During the 1970s over half of the city's shanty towns were upgraded (Fig. 5.11) under the West Bengal Slum Areas (Improvement and Clearance) Bill. Provision was made for landowners to be bought out and for basic amenities to be provided: paved paths; storm drains; a clean water supply; and building brick toilet blocks with proper sewerage. C.M.D.A. also planned the building of two new satellite towns outside Calcutta in an attempt to relieve the congestion in the city and direct growth away to other 'planned' areas.

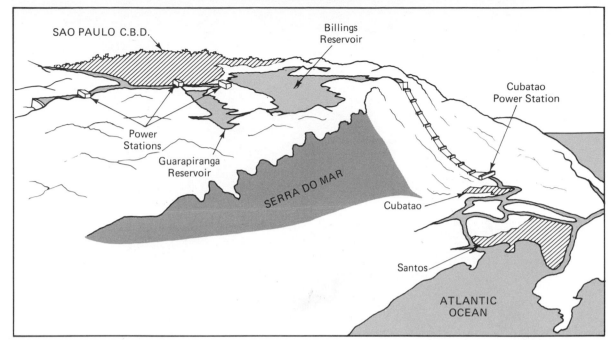

5.13 Location of Sao Paulo

The city's only waterworks, the Pulta works, built in the 1850s, was improved to increase its capacity and new works built at Garden Ridge and Howrah. These schemes, together with the sinking of deep tube wells all over the metropolitan area, has increased the production of much-needed fresh water from 80 million to 250 million gallons per day.

The Development Plan recommended that transport congestion in the city, especially on the one bridge crossing the Hooghly which carries half a million people per day, might be relieved by the building of two new bridges. A network of new roads was also planned and construction of an underground railway was started in an attempt to cut down on the huge traffic jams which occur during the rush hours.

While much progress has been made, lack of money and resources have meant that only parts of the original plan have been carried out. There remains still only one bridge over the Hooghly although a second is under construction. Air pollution remains a major problem with an estimated 60% of the city's residents suffering from respiratory diseases. A 1982 report stated that the Hooghly 'is choked with the untreated industrial wastes from more than 150 major factories around Calcutta. Raw sewage pours into the river continuously from 361 outfalls'. Finally, the underground railway, due to open in 1979 has still to be completed.

Case study: Sao Paulo

Sao Paulo lies within the South East district of Brazil and, with its 15 million population in 1985, was the second largest urban centre, after Mexico City, among the developing countries of the world. Recent estimates suggest that by the year 2000 it could be the second largest city in the world with between 25 and 30 million people. The dramatic growth of the city in this century has brought with it many of the problems associated with rapid urbanization. However, as a result of these problems, especially congestion, crime and pollution, attempts are being made by the metropolitan planning boards to control the city's excessive growth and, in so doing, reduce existing problems.

Sao Paulo was founded near the confluence of the Tiete and Tamanduate rivers some 100 km from the port of Santos and separated from the coast by the great escarpment of the Serra do Mar (Fig. 5.13).

In 1870 Sao Paulo was only a small town of 25 000 people. The first main boost to the population came through the expansion of the coffee industry which attracted migrants and took it to a city of 65 000 by 1890. Industrial growth and **diversification** of the industrial base was stimulated further at the start of the 20th century through the building of the Cubatao hydro electric scheme in 1901 and the development of a highly integrated road and rail transport network throughout the

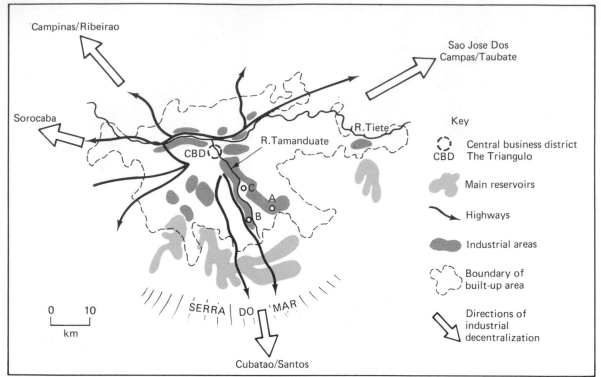

5.14 Greater Sao Paulo

State of Sao Paulo. By 1920 the city had grown to over half a million people and by 1924 it had overtaken Rio de Janiero as the most important industrial centre in Latin America. Much of this industrial development was concentrated along the southern bank of the River Tiete but, such was the pace of industrial growth, that by the 1930s, new industrial areas had been established to the southeast of the city – the 'ABC' complex, along the transport link with Santos (Fig. 5.14). These areas contain many of the chemical, metal and car industries (V.W., Ford, General Motors, Toyota) that epitomise the large-scale industrial developments for which the city is famous. A further boost was given to Sao Paulo's place as Brazil's industrial centre with its selection by the government in the 1950s as an area for priority industrial development.

The rapid industrialization called for considerable investment in machinery, factories and infrastructure and much of this was financed with large amounts of money borrowed from abroad. It was also helped directly by government incentives and import controls which expanded local production of goods. All the time the city's population expanded greatly through natural increase and rapid in-migration of rural dwellers attracted by this 'magnetic' city. Over the 30 year period

between 1950 and 1980 the total population of Sao Paulo State rose from 9.1 million to 25 million while the urban population rose from 4 million to 19.9 million. This urban growth very much reflected the strong underlying growth in the Brazilian economy over this period. National output rose by 7.5% per annum between 1950 and 1975 growing especially fast between 1968 and 1975 – the 'miracle years'. By the late 1970s Sao Paulo State had 19% of Brazil's population yet it accounted for 49% of the country's net industrial product. During the 1970s the industrial success of Sao Paulo was attracting half a million migrants each year and the many ravines along the Tiete and its tributaries had become crowded with the shanty towns (favelas) which housed over 3 million of the migrant population. As in many cities, the favelas of Sao Paulo are characterised by poverty and disease and for most of their populations (favelados) and the city's estimated one million 'street children' the 'economic miracle' has quite simply never happened. Many of the migrant population have never found the employment in Sao Paulo's factories that attracted them there in the first place. As a consequence, many have been forced into working in the **informal sector** of industry, characterised by insecurity and very low incomes, working in menial jobs such as porters, shoeshines and street vendors. A recent survey in Sao Paulo suggested that this 'informal sector' employs over half of the city's population.

Many of the problems and pressures resulting from rapid urbanization – pollution, transport, poor housing and pressures on services – were recognised in the late 1960s and early 1970s and some attempts have since been made to tackle them. The Metropolitan Planning Corporation (EMPLASA) was set up to implement a coherent urban development plan covering housing, industry and transport.

The problem of limited public mobility through Sao Paulo's poor public transport system and congested streets led, in 1975, to the opening of the first phase of the city's underground metro system. Today it carries over 700 000 passengers each day and is being extended in an attempt to further improve passenger movement and reduce pollution throughout the city. Many new highways, such as the Sao Paulo Beltway, have been built within and around the city to improve traffic flow. New train and bus services have been created and large areas of the city centre are now pedestrianized and have parking restrictions.

The National Housing Bank, set up in 1964, has been responsible for providing water and sanitation to shanty town areas and, by 1985, they had constructed a total of 4.5 million new houses throughout Brazil. This 'humanizing' of the shanty towns through the provision of basic amenities and the development of community projects such as skill centres and soup kitchens has improved conditions in some of the favelas. However, the main problem to be overcome in many of the favelas remains the need for residents to have legal ownership to their land for many of the improvements to be effective in the long-term.

A major feature of the planning policies for Sao Paulo has been the industrial 'decentralization' of the metropolitan area along four major axes in an attempt to restrain future growth in the city area and promote industrial development in smaller centres. (Fig. 5.14).

Axis 1 Campinas/Ribeirao – traditionally had industries based on food processing but newer industries include car parts and tractors.

Axis 2 Sorocaba – traditional industries included textiles and food processing. Abundant H.E.P. has led to the development of aluminium smelting.

Axis 3 Cubatao/Santos – new industries include petrochemicals and an integrated steel works at Cubatao. Santos is Brazil's major port.

Axis 4 Sao Jose dos Campos/Taubate – running along the Paraiba valley and linking Sao Paulo with Rio de Janiero. Newer industries include air-

	1950/60	1960/70	1970/80
SÃO PAULO METROPOLITAN AREA	5.4	6.0	4.4
BRAZIL (Urban)	5.6	5.4	4.4
BRAZIL (Total)	3.0	2.9	2.5

5.15 Urban population growth rates (%) for Brazil

craft, pharmaceuticals and car components.

This policy of industrial 'decentralization' has met with some success. This success, together with a slowing of in-migration and a drop in the underlying rate of natural increase, is reflected in a fall in Sao Paulo's rate of urban growth (Fig. 5.15). A number of 'push' factors have contributed towards this success in moving industry away from congested Sao Paulo. Firstly, a shortage of land and strict zoning restrictions together with the rising price of industrial land have forced many new industries to locate outside the city. Secondly, industrial pollution controls were introduced in 1976 to cover new factories and extended in 1980 to include existing factories and, with licences easier to obtain outside the Greater Sao Paulo area, industry has been diverted away to new areas. There have also been some 'pull' factors encouraging 'decentralization' of industry. The development of the fuel–alcohol programme which is designed to replace gasoline for vehicles with alcohol made from sugar cane has generated extensive investment in distilleries in the agricultural regions of Sao Paulo State thus changing the opportunities for migrant farm workers. Also, there has been an improvement in the availability and quality of housing and the industrial infrastructure outside the metropolitan area. By 1980 over 80% of all rural households in Sao Paulo State had electricity, 75% had piped water and over half were linked to the sewerage network. On these indices, the rural households were, on average, better off than those in metropolitan Sao Paulo.

Added to all of these aspects of the 'decentralization' programme is the fact that, since 1982, Brazil's economy has entered a deep recession with G.N.P. falling back and industrial production well down on past levels. It has become the largest debtor country in the world owing $102 billion to other countries and individual banks in 1984. The ending of the 'miracle' has meant that over 800 000 jobs have been lost in Sao Paulo alone and the crime rate in the city has rocketed. One in three citizens are estimated to have been assaulted and there are, on average, 30 bank robberies each month. All of this unrest led to mass rioting at the high cost of living.

The various policies aimed at limiting Sao Paulo's growth and solving some of the problems caused by rapid urbanization have all had their limited successes. However, Sao Paulo remains as Brazil's largest city and main industrial centre and, as such, will continue to attract rural migrants in the future. Continued investment in these urban policies will be necessary to ensure that housing, industry and transport can all cope at even a basic level with this population influx and natural increase. However, investment in rural policies is now underway in an attempt to reduce in-migration to the city and improve conditions in the countryside.

15. For either Calcutta or Sao Paulo outline the main factors which have encouraged migration, the main problems that have arisen from its rapid growth and the attempted solutions.

Urbanization – the developed world

Fig. 5.2 shows that the process of rapid urbanization started much earlier in the developed countries of the world than in the developing countries. Fig. 5.1 points to the fact that, although the rate of urbanization is now much slower in the more developed countries, it is in these areas that the greatest urban population percentages are to be found today and are likely to be found in the future. As a consequence, many of the large cities in developed countries have exhibited, for many years, problems surprisingly similar to those found today in the rapidly urbanizing cities of the third world – traffic congestion, pollution, slum housing, crime, pressures on public and social services and lack of space. Nowhere is this more apparent than in New York, part of a huge **megalopolis** stretching from Boston through Philadelphia and Baltimore to Washington D.C. The cities of this 'Bos-Wash' megalopolitan area cover only some 2% of the total land area of the U.S. but contained in 1985 over 50 million people, one-fifth of the total U.S. population.

Case study: New York

Like that of many large cities of the developed world, New York's central city population has shown a decrease over the past decade although the areal extent of the city and its overall population have grown through suburbanization. The population of this large city and its industries create many pressures on services. For example, the 23 000 tonnes of rubbish produced daily (7 million tonnes each year) need collecting, and the need for 1.5 billion gallons of water each day entails transporting water from up to 500 km away. The many people and large companies that have moved away from the centre of the city obviously no longer pay towards the high cost of maintaining services. This has led to the threat of bankruptcy facing the city each year. It also means there are fewer financial resources to help solve the problems of urban decay and crime found in many of the inner city areas such as Harlem and Bedford-Stuyvesant – **ghettos** where many Puerto Rican, Negro, Italian and other ethnic minority families live. The 'melting pot' of many races that is New York city, with its concentration of a variety of ethnic groups around the city centre, all suffering from relative poverty, high unemployment, poor facilities and 'slum' living conditions, has created much social unrest and tension and this has led to street riots in the city since 1967.

Although many people have moved away from the city over 2 million still commute daily to the C.B.D. creating additional problems of traffic congestion and pollution. It is estimated that over 100 million cars annually pass through New York's tunnels and across its bridges and many new expressways have had to be built helping to ease traffic flow but adding considerably to the city's environmental problems. The city's 370 km of subway has also helped to ease commuter flow but it has become infamous in recent years for vandalism and crime with 13 870 serious subway crimes in 1984. Added to these serious crimes are the 350 000 others that take place on average on the city's streets each year and the five murders which occur every day. Some of the blame for the dramatic increase in crime has been put on the city's increased unemployment as older industries and services have declined and other **footloose industries** have moved to suburban locations.

In few cities of the world are the problems of urbanization so dramatically visible as in New York. In an attempt to ensure that similar problems do not arise many urban areas have developed and implemented long-term planning strategies using the relatively greater financial resources available to them than to urban centres of the third world. One such area is Randstad Holland.

Case study: Randstad Holland

Randstad is a term which originated in the 1930s for the 50–60 km crescent of towns and cities lying close together in the west of the Netherlands (Fig. 5.16). Literally translated the word means 'rim city' although it is wrong to think of Randstad as a single city or indeed as a complete ring since it is

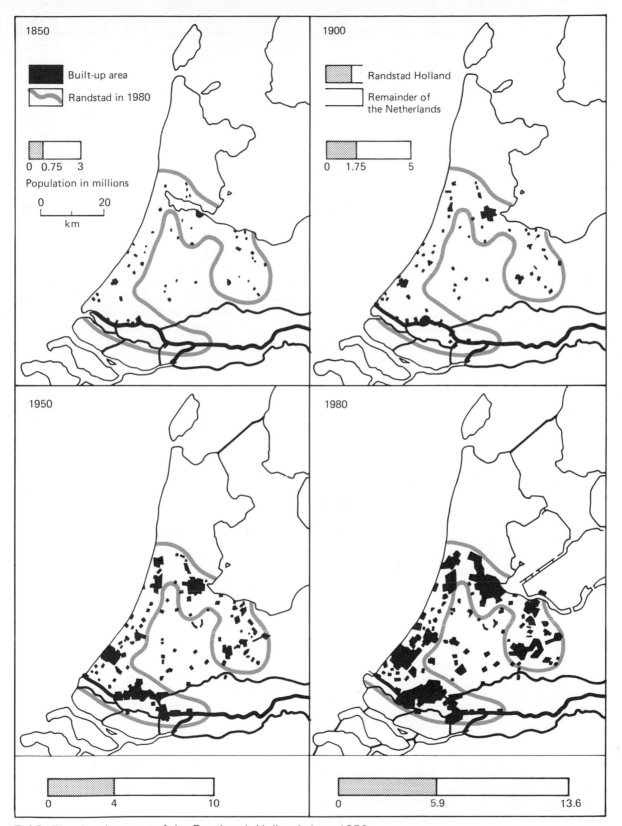

5.16 The development of the Randstad, Holland since 1850

Within the figure:

- 1850
  - Built-up area
  - Randstad in 1980
  - 0   0.75   3
  - Population in millions
  - 0   20
  - km

- 1900
  - Randstad Holland
  - Remainder of the Netherlands
  - 0   1.75   5

- 1950
  - 0   4   10

- 1980
  - 0   5.9   13.6

not fully complete in the south-east. Rather, it is made up of two main areas:

(a) the crescent-shaped rim of urban area consisting of many towns and cities and which, in 1986, had a population density of nearly 1000 people/km^2, one of the highest in W. Europe;

(b) the 'Green Heart' of predominantly rural character with areas used for livestock and arable farming, horticulture and open air recreation. It is because of the growing effect of urban activities on rural areas (traffic, recreation and **suburbanization**) that this 'Green Heart' is considered as part of the overall Randstad region.

Within this part of the Netherlands there was rapid industrial development and housing construction immediately following the Second World War. As in many W. European countries there was a post-war 'bulge' in the birth rate. Much of this growth was concentrated in the main cities of Amsterdam, The Hague, Rotterdam and Utrecht which by 1960 had become highly urbanized areas with 45% of the total population of all the western Netherlands area. Large-scale housing developments and industrial growth expanded the built-up areas considerably throughout the 1950s and 1960s (Fig. 5.16) and this created serious problems of congestion, a high population density, lack of space and the 'infilling' of the 'Green Heart' with the encroachment of suburban development

In order to overcome some of these problems caused by rapid urbanization a series of planning reports published from 1960 onwards made three major recommendations:

(a) Major cities should be permanently separated by 'buffer zones' of open farmland.

(b) The 'Green Heart' should be safeguarded from further urban encroachment which would mean a loss of valuable farmland and recreational space.

(c) Some **'overspill'** population and industrial development should be 'dispersed' to other parts of the Netherlands.

In the 1966 report much emphasis was placed on finding a solution to the continuing process of suburbanization which threatened to complete the urban ring and fill in the 'Green Heart'. The proposed solution was to have a policy of 'concentrated deconcentration' which suggested that the part of the population increase which took place outside the major cities should be accommodated in a limited number of places which were not too small in size and at not too great a distance from the central Randstad cities. The idea behind

this policy was to counter the disadvantage of having too much deconcentration resulting in loss of farmland, a large number of small places with low levels of services, and overconcentration in a few very large cities leading to a poor living environment and congestion. Also, in the early 1970s the Dutch government attempted various other ways to 'disperse' population and industrial development away from Randstad. Subsidies, levies and licences were introduced to slow down industrial investment in some parts and encourage it in others. Government departmental offices underwent large-scale dispersal from The Hague.

However, lack of effective powers for carrying out these policies meant that they had only minimal success in halting the growth and spread of Randstad. In spite of 'concentrated deconcentration' the 'Green Heart' continued to become suburbanized. Many government civil servants continued to live in the same place and simply travelled a greater distance to their 'dispersed' office. The economic recession of the 1970s meant that there was little money for investment in industry in 'dispersed' areas.

During the 1970s, however, plans for the dispersal of development from Randstad had to be revised as a result of several developments. Firstly, the birth rate had suddenly begun to fall so that population projections of 20 million by 2000 had to be dramatically revised to 14–15 million. Secondly, the population of the cities was seen to be falling with all four major centres having large drops in population between 1969 and 1979 (Fig. 5.17). This was due mainly to continued suburbanization, especially in the 'Green Heart' area and in areas of attractive landscape to the east, as 'push' factors in the cities and 'pull' factors in the rural areas operated. This loss of city population was a major cause for concern as it had profound consequences on levels of services and threatened the economic,

Population (000s)	1969	1979	increase %
Amsterdam	845 8	718 6	−15.0
Rotterdam	699 2	582 4	−16.7
The Hague	563 6	458 2	−18.7
Utrecht	276 3	236 1	−14.5
Haarlem	172 9	159 7	− 7.6
Dordrecht	97 0	106 1	+ 9.4
Leiden	102 5	102 7	+ 0.2
Hilversum	100 4	93 4	− 7.0
Delft	81 6	83 7	+ 2.6

5.17 Population of the towns in the Ranstad

social and cultural significance of Randstad on the international scene. Thirdly, increasing prosperity and mobility had provided the opportunity for living more pleasantly and cheaply away from the cities in housing areas built at a much lower density. As a result there was a rapid growth in commuting over increasingly long distances at a time when concern was growing for levels of pollution and conservation of the environment.

Following these developments of the early and mid 1970s, the Urbanization Report was produced in 1977. It suggested a totally new approach to the development of Randstad – an 'anti dispersal' policy. It also contained much more detailed plans for the future form of this urban area. No longer were indications given in only vague terms of where future developments were to take place, but precise sites were named, together with the number of houses to be built. Also, the Report was much more specific about the legal powers to be used to achieve the proposed goals.

The main proposal of the Urbanization Report was that migration from the cities should be stopped. It recommended that areas of the cities such as old housing areas and derelict, empty land sites should be redeveloped with new dwellings and congestion reduced so improving the living environment within the cities, encouraging people to stay or even to return. It also suggested that any

population leaving the cities should be accommodated in a limited number of growth towns and growth centres preferably in the western Randstad area and at a short distance from the major cities thus reducing commuting and pollution (Fig. 5.18). Designation as a growth centre means that at least 6000 houses have to be built within a ten year period. For growth towns the corresponding figure is 10 000. To aid this proposal, financial support is offered by the Dutch government. The Report also gives a more positive function to the 'buffer zones'. Initially these were seen as being open areas used only as a method of separating neighbouring urban areas. With the increase in leisure and recreation over the past decade, many **buffer zones** are being laid out as areas for open air recreation, located near to the main urban centres. One such major buffer zone is the 2700 ha Spaarnwoude area located between Amsterdam and Haarlem which offers a large variety of active and passive recreational pursuits. A similar project is proposed for a 6000 ha area known as 'Midden – Delfland' between Rotterdam, Delft and The Hague.

16. 'Problems of urban development are largely confined to the inner city in developed countries, while in developing countries they tend to occur on the outskirts'. Discuss with examples.

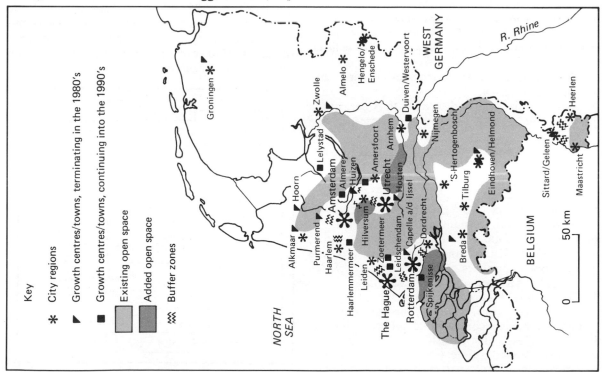

5.18 Structure plan of the Netherlands – 1984

6

Migration – a world on the move

Migration is the word generally used to describe any movement of population. Its study is important in geography since the size and structure of a country's population is affected not only by natural gain and loss resulting from births and deaths, but by the movements of people into the country (**immigrants**) and out of the country (**emigrants**). The difference between the number of permanent immigrants and emigrants produces the net migration of a country.

The movement of population is something that has existed since early times. Prehistoric tribes had to be constantly on the move in their search for food, following and hunting animals and gathering plants. Even today, tribes of people such as Inuits and Aborigines perform similar migrations as part of their established lifestyle. Until the 16th century, migration of population was on a fairly small scale. Since then the rise of towns and cities and the development of industry has led to some major mass movements of population such as those listed below.

1. From Spain and Portugal to South America and Central America.
2. Slaves from West Africa to South America, the West Indies and the southern states of the U.S.A.
3. From the eastern seaboard of the U.S.A. westwards to the Great Plains and the Pacific coast.
4. From western Russia eastwards to Siberia and the Pacific coast.
5. From Europe to the U.S.A., Canada, Australia, New Zealand and South Africa.
6. From developing countries such as India, China, Pakistan and Bangladesh to the developed countries of N.W. Europe, U.S.A., Canada, Australia and New Zealand.
7. Worldwide refugee migrations.

Over the centuries, however, the movements of population have become exceedingly complex and it is possible to distinguish variations in cause (voluntary/forced), time (short-term/long-term), distance (internal/international), scale (individual/mass) and effect.

At the one extreme were the mass, permanent migrations of the 19th century from Europe to North America, Oceania, South Africa and parts of South America. These population movements were mainly voluntary and it is estimated that over 50 million people emigrated from Europe between 1840 and 1930 to settle in these new lands. A century before, between 1700 and 1815, a similar mass migration, this time forced, took place as over 10 million African slaves from Angola, Ghana and Nigeria were transported across the Atlantic to the Americas. Another extreme of migration is the daily, recurring movements of the **commuter** travelling a relatively short distance to and from work each day and the voluntary migrations of the holidaymaker, a movement which has increased dramatically over the last 30 years and which involved some 286 million 'migrations' worldwide in 1983. It is because of these many differences and variables that migrations of people are so difficult to classify. However, Fig. 6.1 suggests four main types of population movement.

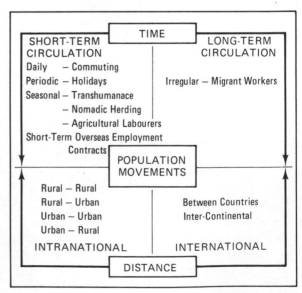

6.1 Classification of population movements

Short-term circulation – The essential feature here is that all movements which take place involve an eventual return to the original location usually after a fairly short period of time. Short-term circulation may involve the migration of complete families but, more commonly involves individuals from within a family.

Long-term circulation involves the movement of people over a greater distance generally between countries or even continents. The migration is, however, only semi-permanent as migrants, after staying within a country for several years, may then return to their country of origin. Such long-term circulation is as likely to involve whole families as it does individuals.

Intranational migrations take place within the boundaries of one particular country and generally involve population movements between urban and rural areas within that country.

International migrations – The important feature is the great distance that is usually involved and the fact that no return is planned or expected. Such movements of population are usually regarded as final and can be brought about by force or a voluntary decision to move.

1.   What is meant by migration?

2.   Look at the following examples of migration. Fit each into the correct category of migration shown in Fig. 6.1:
   (a) movement of rural families to live in Lima, Peru;
   (b) 1960–85 movement from new commonwealth (India, Pakistan, Bangladesh, Nigeria, West Indies) to Britain;
   (c) 36 400 Italians move to work in Switzerland in 1983;
   (d) 6.75 million holidaymakers visit the Caribbean in 1983;
   (e) 1972 27 000 British Asians expelled from Uganda to resettle in Britain.

Causes and effects of migration

The factors which cause a person to move are many and varied but they are usually complementary and due to 'push' and 'pull' factors such as those discussed in Chapter 5. A decision to move is usually based on the perceived advantages and disadvantages of the place of origin and the destination together with consideration of intervening obstacles such as cost and distance and personal factors such as qualifications and family ties.

However, the 'push-pull' theory has been criticised as being too simplistic. It is said to place too much emphasis on economic and demographic features and less on personality factors such as the simple wish to travel and see other places. It has also been suggested that the theory is of less use in the contemporary world since it tends to emphasise migration as an uncommon activity. Indeed, geographers are now suggesting that in our society today it may be more realistic to question why people stay in one place rather than why they move. However, the 'push-pull' theory of migration is a good starter for the study of migration and what is important is the realisation that the movement of people affects not only the population of the destination but also that of the place of origin. At the same time, the structure of the population in both place of origin and destination change too. The many and varied movements of population can, therefore, have profound social, political, economic and environmental effects on and within origin and destination points.

Recurring movement such as commuting to work in city centres creates crowded, congested areas and acute environmental problems by day. These same areas may be almost deserted by night. At the same time, the suburbs experience corresponding changes in daily population. Similarly holiday resorts which attract large populations benefit economically during the holiday season, but they can be almost empty at other times of the year. The famous exodus of Glasgow's population from the city to coastal resorts such as Dunoon, Rothesay and Saltcoats during the 'Glasgow Fair' holiday created a dramatic drop in the city's population for the fortnight holiday period. Even today there is a noticeable, temporary drop in population numbers during this holiday period although destinations receiving the swell of people and the economic benefits have changed markedly.

In many cases population movements can be 'age selective' creating specific problems for the place of origin and the destination. The out-migration of young people from an area can leave it with an ageing and declining workforce with a high proportion of old people dependent on those younger people that remain (Fig. 6.2).

As a consequence of such a movement, services such as transport and shops may be reduced, homes may be abandoned, jobs may be lost and a general decline set in. This in turn may even increase the prospect of further out-migration from the area. Such a situation, common in many parts of the Scottish Highlands and Islands until the mid 1960s may need political intervention in order to arrest any social, economic and environmental decline in such areas. In some movements of population it can be mainly older people who are involved. On

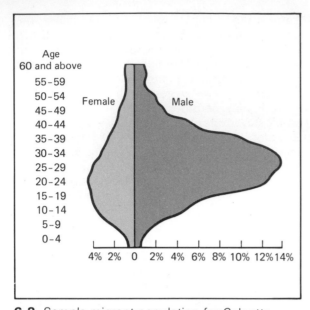

6.2 Sample migrant population for Calcutta

reaching retirement age some people decide to move and areas such as the south coast of England, parts of Florida and, more recently, Spain have become especially popular with the resultant preponderance of elderly people in the population structures of those areas and the need for appropriate services to cater for this.

The movement of populations across international boundaries either in the form of 'forced' refugees or migrant workers from developing countries to developed countries and between developing countries can have a significant impact on international relations. It can also raise sensitive political issues and create problems of social assimilation. Such a movement into a country of new migrants can bring economic benefits such as an expanding market and labour force, not least in the unattractive jobs shunned by the indigenous population.

The receiving country also benefits as migrant workers tend to make manufacturing industries in the host country more competitive with costs in the construction and service industries being kept down. At the same time, however, such in-migration on a large and persistant scale can cause considerable pressures on social services such as hospitals, schools and housing and friction can be created as cultural and social minority groups attempt to adjust to life in a new country.

Skilled migrants such as doctors, scientists, teachers and engineers are particularly valuable to a receiving country as they save their host country substantial costs in education and training. Such a movement of skilled persons was especially com-

mon in the 1960s and 1970s when many moved from developing to more developed countries. The main sending countries have been India, Pakistan, Sri Lanka and the Philippines with many going to the U.S.A., Canada and Britain. Within Britain in recent years there has been a **'brain drain'** of skilled labour to the Midlands and the south of England attracted by the employment prospects. Skilled British workers have also migrated temporarily and permanently overseas for similar reasons with the figure reaching 164 000 in 1984. This 'brain drain' of skilled and professional migrants presents obvious problems to the sending country especially if the migration is permanent. It is possible, however, for such migrations to have a very positive effect on the sending country. Many migrants return home with additional skills which can benefit their country. Also, many migrants send money back home to their family and relations still living in the sending country. In 1985 over $7 billion was sent from Western Europe and nearly $5 billion from the countries of the Middle East to the countries of migrant workers. In some developing countries these foreign earnings can match or even surpass the country's export earnings from commodities and manufactures.

This international migration of population from developing to developed countries has undergone considerable changes in recent years brought on mainly by the 1973 world oil crisis and the economic recession of the past decade. Many countries such as Australia, U.S.A., Canada and the countries of north-west Europe, who until the early 1970s attracted and even encouraged millions of migrants from developing countries, have now introduced strict controls on the number of immigrants allowed to settle permanently. For example, between 1966 and 1974 foreign migrants to France increased by a rate of 40% but this rate of increase was only 9% between 1974 and 1982. In spite of some degree of success with immigration bans and restrictions, the total number of foreign residents in developed countries has shown little signs of any dramatic drop. For example, between 1974 and 1982 France's total immigrant population remained at about 4 million. This has been due to the increase in numbers of migrant family members who accompanied the workers and the relatively higher rate of natural increase among existing, settled migrant groups. The fact that many of these foreign residents have tended to be unskilled and employed in traditionally low paid jobs such as transport, labouring and more menial services has created a major cause for concern in some countries (Fig. 6.3).

Occupations	Italians	Spanish	Portuguese	Other EEC	Turks	Algerians	Moroccans	Tunisians
Farmers	3.1	1.2	X	6.4	X	X	X	X
Farm workers	2.7	8.2	3.2	3.1	4.8	X	15.2	4.5
Professional and managerial	11.9	6.6	1.5	38.7	2.6	3.9	3.6	8.9
Skilled workmen and apprentices	33.6	27.2	26.0	12.1	19.6	19.2	15.0	23.7
Unskilled workers	33.9	34.8	55.4	14.3	70.8	67.2	56.1	58.1
Domestic and other services	5.2	14.6	10.2	5.0	X	2.5	3.1	3.4
Others	9.6	7.3	3.6	20.3	1.9	6.2	6.9	7.7

X = less than 1 per cent

6.3 Occupation groups of immigrants to France

In times of recession it has not always been these types of jobs that have been lost and so it has not always been immigrants that have been made redundant. All of this, together with increasing unemployment, not least among young, second generation immigrants, has led to growing social tension and unrest between migrant groups and an increasingly resentful host population. The repatriation of migrant workers and their families from developed countries as a result of economic recession can have a devastating effect on their country of return. This '**return migration**', which effectively means exporting unemployment back to the countries of origin creates a sudden increase in unemployment in the country of origin and a sharp decrease in income, both of which can lead to major social, economic and political problems thus adding to the burden of a developing country.

As a result of such barriers to free migration there has, in recent years, been a considerable increase in the number of attempted illegal migrations between countries, especially from developing to developed countries. Nowhere is this more apparent than along the border between Mexico and the U.S.A. where illegal entry can even be organized at a price by traffickers in the sending and receiving country. These illegal migrants may find some employment, generally in the 'dirty' job sector of the economy, but they can also add to the pressures on public and social services in the area to which they move. Many are also forced to live in areas of very low quality housing which can lead to overcrowding and other environmental problems generally attributed to the shanty towns of the third world.

3. Make a list of some of the problems and advantages arising from the loss and gain of population resulting from migration.

4. Describe the type of employment generally undertaken by migrant workers in their host country.

Short term circulation

Commuting

Daily migration such as commuting to work in urban centres is generally over a fairly small distance. In the U.K. the most common commuting distance is between 5 and 10 km although around London the zone from which daily commuters travel extends to over 150 km from the city and can involve commuters in car, bus or train journeys of over 2 hours in each direction. Fig. 6.4 shows the commuting areas for selected major towns and cities in the U.K. The scale of commuter migration in the U.K. is best seen when one considers that in 1981 37% of the men in employment and 25% of the women in employment worked outside the local authority district in which they lived. These proportions vary widely over the country with Greater London having the highest proportions for both men and women at 60% and 48% respectively. Areas with the lowest rates of commuting where fewer than 20% of the residents worked in another local authority district tended to be in remote and rural areas in Wales, west and south-west England and north and west Scotland.

However, what the figures amount to is a daily commuter migration of over 17 million people in the U.K. With half of them travelling by car, 16% by bus and 6% by train or tube the resultant problems created by this mass movement such as peak hour demand, congestion and rush hours are easily understood (Fig. 6.5).

Within the U.K. these problems caused by mass commuting are best seen in the London area where every working day 1.07 million workers crowd the 10 miles^2 of the central city with just a further 2.6

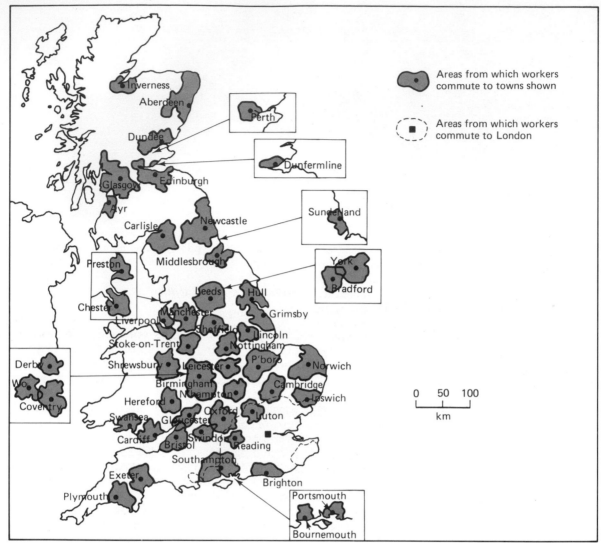

6.4 Commuter areas in the U.K.

million workers in the rest of Greater London's 610 miles².

Within the large urban centres of the U.S. the distances covered by daily commuters tend to be greater than in the U.K. Also, considerably more move by car and this has affected land-use in cities, much of which has had to be given over to catering for motor vehicles. For example, it is estimated that in central Los Angeles over 70% of the land is taken up by freeways, roads and car parking areas needed to cope with the daily influx of commuter traffic. One unfortunate outcome of this mass daily movement by car is the blanket of **smog** which envelops the city and its surroundings, especially in the summer (Fig. 6.6). Smog pollution is caused by the action of sunlight on reactive hydrocarbons and oxides of nitrogen and in Los Angeles vehicles are responsible for over 80% of the emissions. This air pollution has necessitated political legislation in the form of Clean Air Acts and the introduction of strict vehicle emission controls. In the Los Angeles basin, these emission controls have reduced the air pollution but smog alerts are still declared from time to time. In September 1979 the Los Angeles basin experienced its worst smog period with 10 days of severe air pollution causing citizens to complain of eye irritation and burning, sore throats and a 50% increase in hospital admissions for chronic lung diseases such as emphysema and asthma. At this level of smog pollution certain industries must reduce their output, air conditioning has to be switched off, school children are kept indoors and commuters are asked to share transport to work.

6.5 Peak hour congestion, London

6.6 Smog, Los Angeles

In many Mediterranean cities such as Rome and Athens, the congestion and air pollution created by commuter traffic is made considerably worse by the added commuter movements caused by the traditional afternoon siesta giving twice as many rush hours as in most other countries. At the same time, the resultant pollution from traffic in these cities has had, and is still having, a harmful effect on the tourist industry and the many ancient buildings found in the cities.

5. Explain why commuting distances have generally increased over the last 30 years.

6. Use Fig. 6.4 to help you explain the commuting areas of London, Birmingham and Glasgow.

Long term circulation

Foreign workers in West Germany

In common with many Western European countries, West Germany's industrial growth has led to many foreign migrants moving to the country either entering or seeking employment. West Germany's need for foreign labour rose considerably in the 1950s with the country having a low birth rate, a stable population, the closure of West Berlin migration routes from East Germany and an increased unwillingness of West Germans to engage in unskilled or menial employment. To remedy this and ensure continued economic prosperity in-migration of foreign workers was actively encouraged with the opening of nearly 400 recruitment offices in many Mediterranean countries such as Turkey, Italy, Yugoslavia, Greece, Spain and Portugal. German employers interviewed and screened potential migrant workers who, if accepted, signed a contract to work in West Germany as a **guestworker** (gastarbeiter). Many of these migrant labour recruits were young, 71%

were male and nearly 90% worked at manual jobs. The annual flow of gastarbeiter, which was 50 000 in 1958, rose to over half a million by the mid 1960s and exceeded 700 000 per year by 1970. Since the economic recession of 1973, however, the West German government has imposed a ban on the recruitment of foreign workers and the former flood of incoming migrant labour has fallen to a trickle in the 1980s (Fig. 6.7). Indeed, as early as 1975 the authorities took measures to ensure a halt to the immigration of foreigners to the cities and counties of Bavaria and Baden-Wurttemberg with foreign populations of over 12%. This early policy of curtailing and directing foreign migrants was said to prevent the 'concentration' of foreign workers and was added to in 1977 when a total of 45 cities including West Berlin, Hanover, Cologne, Munich and Frankfurt began to actively prevent further immigration of foreign workers.

However, total numbers of foreign workers within the country and total numbers of foreign population have not declined quite as much as the West German government had expected for reasons already mentioned, together with an increase in applications for political asylum and the fact that even on becoming unemployed many foreign workers, especially Turks and Italians, have tended to remain in the country rather than return home. This has been because unemployment in countries of origin has generally been higher than that of West Germany. Today, West Germany has a total foreign population of 4.7 million making up nearly 8% of the country's total population and the gradual development of this large, multi-ethnic group, resulting initially from in-migration, has presented the West German authorities with many social and economic problems.

The question of migrant workers and their families living in West Germany is something that the West German media have devoted a large amount of time to during the early and mid 1980s as

NATIONALITY	1974	1975	1976	1977	1978	1979	1980	1981	1982
AUSTRIA	7.4	3.3	4.3	5.3	3.8	6.8	10.4	9.3	5.6
GREECE	1.8	0.7	0.8	1.1	0.8	0.8	0.9	0.5	0.3
SPAIN	1.2	0.5	0.7	0.4	0.3	0.2	0.5	1.1	0.7
SWITZERLAND		0.6	0.6	0.6	0.3	0.5	0.6	0.5	0.5
TURKEY	6.1	2.0	2.6	3.3	1.5	5.7	29.2	3.6	0.4
YUGOSLAVIA	7.7	3.0	2.1	2.8	2.6	5.7	7.9	5.1	3.3
OTHERS	19.4	11.8	13.0	16.2	10.2	18.2	33.1	23.1	15.1
TOTAL INFLOW	43.6	21.9	24.1	29.7	19.5	37.9	82.6	43.9	25.9
Total Foreign Workers	2387	2227	2027	1978	1962	2014	2169	2082	2038
Total Foreign Population	4127	4090	3948	3948	3981	4144	4453	4630	4667

6.7 Foreign migrant workers to W. Germany – 1974–82 (thousands)

it is seen as a source of conflict and the catalyst to street riots in some cities during 1983. Migrant workers view themselves as victims of discrimination, especially at work, but also in accommodation, public services and education. The conflict appears to have arisen because many native Germans are concerned at increasing unemployment (9.1% in 1984) and the resultant social security and social benefit problems this and an increasingly youthful and aged dependent population will bring in years to come. The large number of foreign juveniles entering the job market is seen as a cause for some concern as it is projected that it will not peak until the late 1980s with over 82 000 second generation youths of foreign migrants looking for employment. The large number of immigrants and their families living within the country has also presented the authorities with the problem of how best and to what extent they should and can be integrated with the host populaion. Successful integration depends very much on education and training, especially in language proficiency, and there is some hope that the increase in numbers of second generation foreign children will make them more proficient in the German language and ease integration.

In response to the growing problems surrounding migrants and their families the West German government attempted in 1982 to limit immigration even further by prohibiting immigration of certain people including 16–17 year olds and foreign children with only one parent in the country. At the same time, migrants are now encouraged to return to their country of origin through the offer of financial incentives, a scheme tried in France in the 1970s. These attempts to 'repatriate' migrants involve the payment of £2500 for each working adult and £360 for each child who leaves the country. Over 80% of the initial applications for repatriation have come from Turks who make up one-third of West Germany's foreign population although the total numbers involved in accepting **repatriation** terms has been well below the 90 000 hoped for by the government.

7. Discuss the reasons for the migration of workers to West Germany in terms of 'push' and 'pull' factors.

8. Why is the West German government keen to 'repatriate' migrant workers and their families?

Intranational migration

Within the basic pattern of population movement into and out of a country, there is also the migration that takes place within the country. The importance of this intranational or internal migration as an aspect of population movement, its causes and effects, can be seen in Britain. Between 1971 and the 1981 census the net population change in the country was a growth of less than 300 000 people or 0.5%. This was in marked contast to the previous decade which saw an increase by over 2.5 million or 5%. What was much more noticeable, however, during the decade up to 1981 was the fact that in some areas population change showed a dramatic increase while in others these was a marked decrease. This change was partly due to people being attracted towards or forced to leave areas for economic, social, political and environmental reasons. This pattern of population change between 1971 and 1981 is shown in Fig. 6.8.

The first main feature of intranational population movement in Britain in recent years has been the increasing move of population away from the major built up areas such as Glasgow, Liverpool, Birmingham and London (Fig. 6.9). This trend towards urban depopulation or **counterurbanization** first became apparent during the 1960s with cities like Glasgow losing tens of thousands of its population as densely populated inner city areas were redeveloped and traditional industries declined with overspill population moving to other towns and new towns. This process of population moving away from the large city areas was still taking place between 1971 and 1981 as Fig. 6.10 shows.

Also to be seen in Fig. 6.10 is the fact that many new and expanded towns such as Milton Keynes and Redditch showed considerable population gains over the decade, much of it allied to the establishment of new industries and housing. What was also apparent however, was the continuing 'drift to the south' of the population in Britain as the vast majority of the fastest growing areas between 1971 and 1981 were still to be found in the south and east of the country reflecting the distribution of job opportunities in the country.

Another important population movement that has emerged in recent years has been the acceleration of population growth in the more rural and remote areas. This 'rural renaissance' or 'urban to rural shift' has been not only to rural areas close to the major urban centres but also in rural areas which are relatively remote from traditional metropolitan influences such as central Wales and the

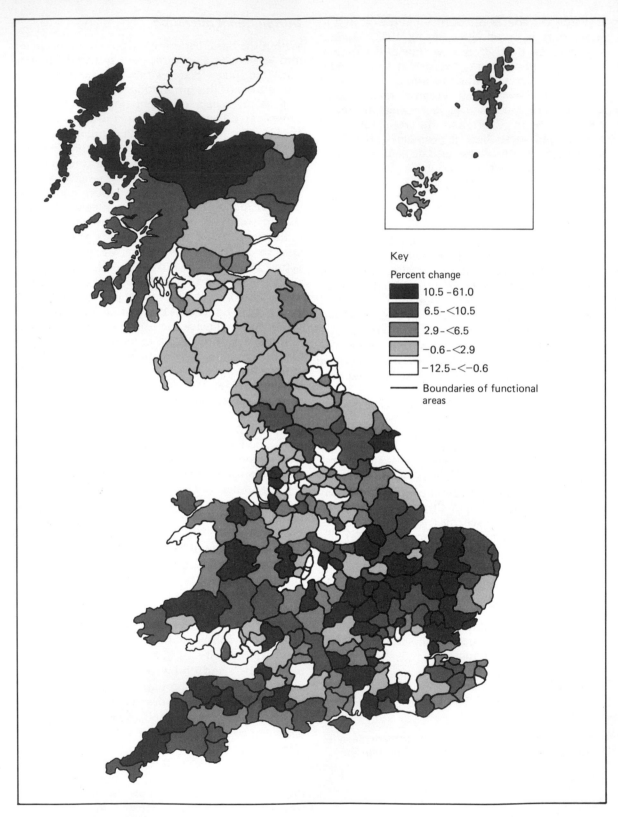

Key

Percent change

- ▉ 10.5 – 61.0
- ▉ 6.5 – <10.5
- ▉ 2.9 – <6.5
- ▉ −0.6 – <2.9
- ▢ −12.5 – <−0.6
- —— Boundaries of functional areas

6.8 Population change in the U.K. – 1971–81

	1911	1931	1951	1961	1971	1981
GREATER LONDON	7160	8110	8197	7992	7452	6696
BIRMINGHAM	526	1003	1113	1107	1015	1007
GLASGOW	784	1088	1090	1055	897	766
LIVERPOOL	746	856	789	746	610	510

6.9 Population of major U.K. cities (thousands) – 1911–81

TEN FASTEST GROWING		TEN FASTEST DECLINING	
	per cent		per cent
Milton Keynes	61	Liverpool	−13
Redditch	50	Glasgow	−12
Tamworth	37	Manchester	−11
Dingwell and Invergordon	34	South Shields	−9
Thetford	30	Sunderland	−9
Bracknell	28	London	−9
Basingstoke	26	Greenock	−7
Huntingdon	25	Peterlee	−6
Widness and Runcorn	24	West Bromwich	−5
Peterborough	23	Consett	−5

6.10 Population change in urban areas – 1971–81

	Population 1981 (thousands)	61–71	71–81	Difference
SCOTLAND	998	−1.9	9.6	+11.5
WALES	583	0.6	6.8	+6.2
NORTH WALES	276	1.0	4.3	+3.3
YORKSHIRE + HUMBERSIDE	453	10.4	12.0	+1.6
EAST MIDLANDS	560	9.2	10.1	+0.9
SOUTH WEST	1368	10.3	11.0	+0.7
WEST MIDLANDS	427	7.7	8.1	+0.4
EAST ANGLIA	1035	14.5	12.9	−1.6
SOUTH EAST	357	21.1	12.1	−9.0
ALL RURAL	6056	7.5	10.2	+2.7

6.11 Population change in rural local authorities – 1961–81

(Convention Relating to the Status of Refugees. The UN High Commissioner for Refugees. 1951.)

Highlands and Islands of Scotland (Fig. 6.11). The increase in population in these areas is largely attributable to the success of agencies such as the Welsh Development Board and the Highlands and Islands Development Board in developing industry in these areas and hence retaining and attracting population. In parts of the Scottish Highlands such as the Shetlands, Grampian and Highland Regions, population has also been attracted by North Sea oil related developments.

9. Use the maps, tables and an atlas to help you describe the extent to which 'counterurbanization' and 'rural renaissance' have taken place in Britain.

10. Explain why they have occurred.

11. Explain why the 'drift to the south' appears to be continuing.

International migration

'A refugee is . . . an individual, who . . . owing to well founded fear of being persecuted for reasons of race, religion, nationality is unable, or, owing to such fear, unwilling to avail himself of the protection of that country; or, who not having a nationality and being outside the country of his former residence as a result of such fear, is unwilling to return to it.'

The international migration of refugees displaced from their home country through religious persecution, war and political upheaval has become such an important feature in world population movement that the Brandt Report described the 20th century as the century of the 'uprooted Man'. Two hundred and fifty million people have fled their country during the century and figures suggest that in 1985 there were between 10–12 million refugees worldwide with an average increase of 2500 every day. Over 25 million refugees were created by the fighting in the Second World War and the subsequent division of large parts of Europe. Ten million people alone moved from Poland and Czechoslovakia into West Germany and nearly 2 million Jews migrated to the new state of Israel. In more recent decades, the focus of the world refugee crisis has turned to the countries of the third world and Africa, which in 1985, harboured about one-half of the world's refugee population with large concentrations in Ethiopia, Zaire and Angola (Fig. 6.12).

Many of these displaced refugees have been forced to flee as a result of civil war and other reasons suggested in the UNHCR definition. However, increasingly, the conditions of dire poverty found in many third world countries and the resultant hopelessness and lack of opportunity has led some people to seek 'refugee' status if possible as a preference to continued life in their present area and conditions. The perception of opportunity as a refugee, no matter how small or unrealistic, has been an important motivating

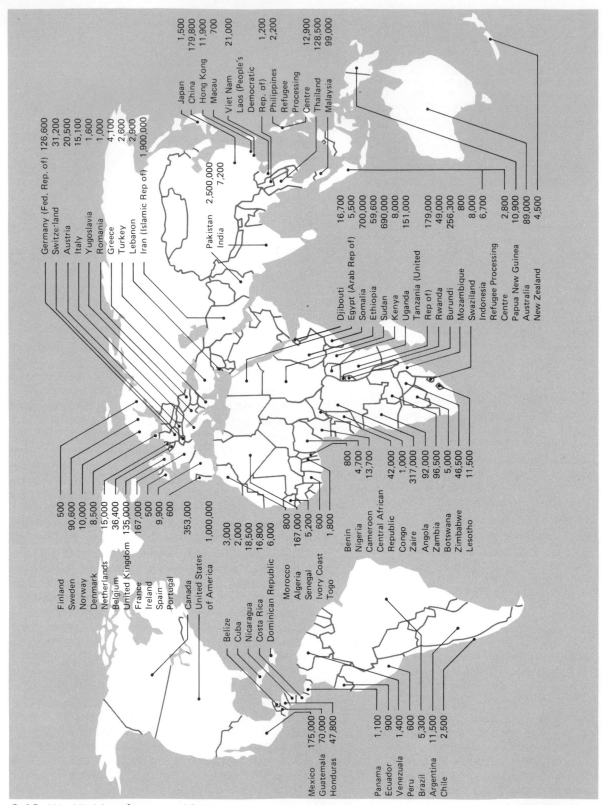

6.12 Worldwide refugees – 1985

factor for many recent 'refugees'. The Universal Declaration of Human Rights states that 'everyone has the right to leave any country, including his own' and that people have 'the right to seek and to enjoy other countries' asylum from persecution'. It falls upon the UNHCR and other international organisations to help look after and protect refugees and their work aims at doing three things:

a) establishing the principle of **asylum** and ensuring that refugees are not forced to return to the country they have fled from;
b) arranging for the care and protection of refugees in temporary asylum;
c) looking for permanent solutions such as voluntary repatriation or resettlement.

It is important to realise that refugee problems are not caused by pressures of population. They result from deep-rooted intolerance, political instability and wars. However, refugees can appear as a problem in many countries since they are dependent on the generosity of the host country and the international community for their immediate survival and longer term economic security. Also, most are concentrated in poorer, third world countries and with them making up over 15% of the population in countries such as Jordan and Somalia, their presence adds considerably to the existing burden placed on services such as health, education, water and employment and resources such as food, land and water. Added to this is often their cultural difference to the host nation which can make successful resettlement and assimilation very difficult.

For the refugees themselves the problems are equally critical since they are foreigners in another country with few rights, limited or uncertain identity and few real prospects. These problems which can arise with the influx of refugees and the reasons behind their initial movement can be seen in the following case study of Vietnam.

Refugees from Vietnam

The war and the changing political circumstances in Indo-China in the 1970s forced over 1.5 million Kampucheans, Laotians and Vietnamese to leave their homes and seek asylum as refugees in other countries. This mass movement of refugees reached a peak in 1979 when nearly 400 000 people arrived in various asylum countries throughout the world. Many left Vietnam, and more recently China, by boat, giving rise to the term 'boat people' and attempted to reach countries such as China, Hong Kong and the Philippines by crossing large sea areas in grossly overcrowded and ill-prepared boats. A large and unknown number of 'boat people' are known to have drowned or starved as they fled the persecution in their homeland but, by the end of 1984 over 1 million refugees from Indo-China had been resettled in over 30 countries throughout the world with the greatest numbers in the U.S.A., France, Australia and Canada (Fig. 6.13).

For many refugees leaving the countries of Indo-China their first landfall was Hong Kong and, on reaching it, they were initially placed in resettlement camps before being granted asylum in another country. Hong Kong itself has officially integrated about 15 000 refugees although in 1986 another 11 000 were still waiting anxiously to learn if they were to be given priority for asylum and resettlement in another country. The presence of such a large number of refugees in a small country which has a population density 20 times that of the U.K. creates obvious problems. Indeed, the prospect of receiving large numbers of refugees in the late 1970s led Thailand to practise its own form of dissuasion by taking boats filled with refugees back out to sea. While resettlement camps, provided by a sympathetic government, offer some form of shelter and security to refugees, many have found their stay in them much longer than they might have anticipated because of their lack of success in being granted asylum in another country. Indefinite stays in such camps with restricted movement cause additional problems of frustration and hopelessness for the refugee population as jobless heads of families gradually lose status and morale and family discipline crumbles. In 1985 there were estimated to be some 160 000 refugees in camps throughout South East Asia the majority being in Thailand. In spite of this, the international effort mounted to grant asylum to refugees in Indo-China has met with some success. Throughout South East Asia, centres have been set up to teach refugees a new language in the hope that many will be potential settlers in western countries. By 1986 over 17 000 had been resettled in Britain. In addition, there is the need for an introduction to the ways of life in these Western countries so that 'culture shock' is lessened. In spite of all this, the successful asylum and resettlement of refugees in a highly technological, urban environment still creates major problems of adjustment for many families. UNHCR have played a major role in resettling refugees giving assistance in integrating, on state farms, over a quarter of a million who fled from Vietnam into the People's Republic of China. They have also helped to coordinate the Orderly Departures Programme from Vietnam in which

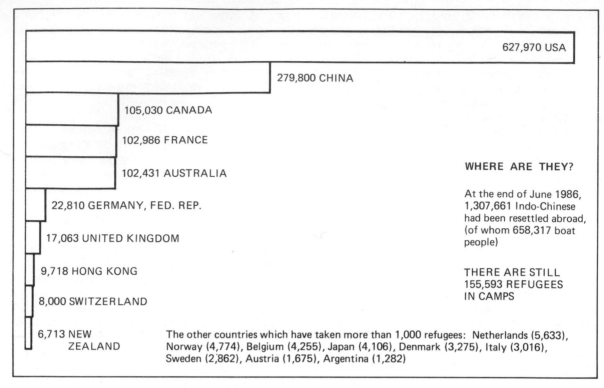

627,970 USA

279,800 CHINA

105,030 CANADA

102,986 FRANCE

102,431 AUSTRALIA

22,810 GERMANY, FED. REP.

17,063 UNITED KINGDOM

9,718 HONG KONG

8,000 SWITZERLAND

6,713 NEW ZEALAND

WHERE ARE THEY?

At the end of June 1986, 1,307,661 Indo-Chinese had been resettled abroad, (of whom 658,317 boat people)

THERE ARE STILL 155,593 REFUGEES IN CAMPS

The other countries which have taken more than 1,000 refugees: Netherlands (5,633), Norway (4,774), Belgium (4,255), Japan (4,106), Denmark (3,275), Italy (3,016), Sweden (2,862), Austria (1,675), Argentina (1,282)

6.13 Refugees from Indo China – 1985

2000 refugees each month are legally permitted to leave the country. Almost 100 000 Vietnamese have been resettled under this scheme and UNHCR have also recently funded a major programme to combat piracy against refugee boats in the South China Sea.

12. Use Fig. 6.12 to help you make a list of the major countries to have received world refugees.

13. Describe some of the programmes that must be implemented to allow successful resettlement of refugees in a foreign country.

International migration – U.K.

Traditionally the U.K. has been a net exporter of population. The first emigrations were associated with the colonization of other nations in Africa, North America and the Far East which began as early as the 16th century. The next major period of emigration got under way in the 1830s with the invention of the steamship which allowed safe and quick ocean crossings for migrants. It is estimated that between 1840 and 1930 over 50 million people emigrated from the U.K. and the rest of Europe to settle in these new lands in North America, New Zealand, Australia, Africa and South America. Fig. 6.14 shows that in 1966 alone over 300 000

people emigrated from the U.K. hoping to start new lives in other countries attracted mainly by better employment prospects and the perception of an improved climate and living standard. In that year Canada and Australia alone took over 63 000 British migrants each, some of whom had been tempted to the latter by the offer of an assisted passage costing only £10 per person. Since 1945 until recently Australia has been the main destination of international British migration. About 1.5 million British have settled there with Canada and New Zealand the next most popular destinations. As with most international migrations, concentrations of migrant populations can be found in the host country. In the case of Australia, the cities of Perth, in Western Australia, and Adelaide have proved to be the most favoured with 15% and 17% of their populations made up of U.K. born people. Even within Adelaide there are very strong concentrations of migrant Britons, with over 50% of both Salisbury and Elizabeth residential areas inhabited by British. Emigrants from Britain to all of these relatively new and expanding countries were initially made up from all occupations – from labourers and skilled tradesmen to doctors and teachers. By the mid 1970s, however, as the world-wide recession took hold, the doors of emigration to Canada, Australia and New Zealand became

YEAR	ALL		AUSTRALIA N.Z., CANADA		INDIA, BANGLADESH, SRI LANKA		CARIBBEAN		E.E.C.		SOUTH AFRICA		PAKISTAN*		MIDDLE EAST		U.S.A.	
	a	b	a	b	a	b	a	b	a	b	a	b	a	b	a	b	a	b
1966	219	302	36	166	27	9	15	9	37	26	7	14					23	27
1971	200	240	52	99	24	8	5	8	21	31	8	21					22	17
1976	191	210	40	63	15	4	4	3	25	31	9	21	12	2			16	21
1978	187	192	34	49	19	4	5	2	24	32	12	4	19	1	13	26	15	25
1979	195	189	31	50	19	4	5	3	23	29	11	6	14	2	14	23	13	26
1980	174	229	23	65	14	5	5	3	23	34	4	11	11	2	13	24	17	29
1981	153	233	20	79	18	2	3	3	23	28	3	23	9	1	11	23	17	25
1982	202	259	20	75	17	5	2	5	54	37	9	27	11	2	11	28	19	30
1983	202	185	32	41	13	4	5	3	31	29	6	9	12	1	13	20	26	32
1984	201	164	28	29	15	3	2	3	22	26	8	9	4	1	11	19	7	28

* Pakistan is included with India, Bangladesh and Sri Lanka until 1972.

6.14 U.K. immigrants (a) and emigrants (b) (thousands) – 1966–84

very firmly closed. In 1984, only 5000 British residents were allowed into Canada. New Zealand accepted about the same number and Australia took 18 000. Even this small number were not allowed in at random since many of the countries have drawn up lists of 'designated occupations'. These lists specify the types of skilled people that are needed in the country and, therefore, most likely to receive priority in being considered for immigration.

However, as some doors have been closed to international migrants leaving the U.K. others have opened. In 1984 the most popular destination for emigrating Britons was the U.S.A. with 28 000, followed by the E.E.C. countries with 26 000 then the Middle East with 19 000, many of which were related to oil exploration and development in the Gulf States. Nowadays, many of these countries insist that potential immigrants must have a guaranteed job and that it must be one for which there are no locally suitable applicants in the host country. One curious fact that has arisen is that according to the U.S. Embassy in London only 5000 immigrant visas are issued to British citizens every year. This does not match with the British Department of Trade's 1984 figures which showed 28 000 Britons emigrating to the U.S.A., even allowing for each visa covering a family group. The inference certainly is that if Britons cannot emigrate to the U.S.A. through official channels then less legal ways are being found!

As a member of the E.E.C. potential British migrants do not need a guarantee of a job in order to move to other member countries. British citizens have the right to seek work in any other Common Market State without a work permit and some British Job Centres will even have details of vacancies in E.E.C. countries. Added to this is the fact that Britons working in the E.E.C. have the same rights as host country nationals over pay, working conditions, housing, social security and trade union membership. All of this has helped make the other countries of the E.E.C. relatively more popular for international emigration from Britain than in the past.

While Britain has lost many people through emigration it has also gained many through immigration (Fig. 6.14). Immediately after the Second World War a great number of European refugees, especially those of Polish origin, entered the country. At the same time, the British economy was recovering from the war and beginning to grow and this created a shortage of workers for factories and services. As a result, immigration, especially from the 'New' Commonwealth, increased considerably. In 1951 there were around 200 000 black people in Britain. Between 1958 and 1962 nearly half a million others had migrated to Britain with a net peak of migration reaching 172 000 in 1961. Many of the immigrants, Indians, Pakistani and West Indians, were a replacement population or workforce filling labour shortages in public transport, cleaning and the health services, doing jobs that the white population no longer wished to do. The vast majority of the immigrants moved to urban centres such as Glasgow, London and Birmingham, concentrating for social and cultural reasons in inner city areas of older, cheaper housing around the city centre vacated by white out-migration and close to the work opportunities of the central city. By 1962, however, a restriction was placed on migration into Britain with the establishment of the Commonwealth Immigrants Act. This Act established a graded system of employment permits which immigrants had to hold to obtain entry. Category 'A' permits were for those who had guaranteed work to go to. 'B' permits were for those migrants with particular skills, such as doctors and nurses, who were needed and 'C' permits were for unskilled workers. Preference was given to 'A' and 'B' categories and 'C' category permits were withdrawn in 1964 with the introduction of even stricter immigration controls. Since the early 1960s the majority of immigrants have been made up of families and dependents of workers already living in Britain. For example, in 1969 there were 36 557 Commonwealth migrants to Britain of which nearly 30 000 were dependents. Immigration was further controlled with the Immigration Act of 1971 and the British Nationality Act 1981, although some relaxation of it was made in 1972 for 27 000 East African Asians forced to leave Uganda by political pressure. By 1977 the total black population of Britain stood at 1.85 million of whom about 40% were born in Britain. By 1984 immigration from the New Commonwealth had dwindled to 24 800 with most being dependent children and wives. Today, as Fig. 6.14 shows, more migrants come from the white Commonwealth countries and those of the E.E.C. Within the U.K. there has been much successful integration of the various waves of migrants over the years. However, racial disadvantage, especially in employment, housing and education led to civil disorder and riots in the 1980s in inner city areas such as St Pauls (Bristol), Brixton and Tottenham (London), Toxteth (Liverpool), Moss Side (Manchester) and Handsworth (Birmingham), and these have served to highlight some of the problems still faced by Britain's multi-ethnic society.

14. Use Fig. 6.14 to help describe some of the main features of U.K. migration since 1966.

15. 'Immigrants are often vilified as society's scapegoat, subjected to harsh immigration restrictions when the demand for labour declines'. Discuss.

16. Using examples from the various case studies discuss the socio-economic problems that arise in a host country as a result of large-scale immigration.

7
Trade or aid – the path to development?

This chapter investigates the competing ideas of using trade and/or aid as a means for development.

Aid

International **aid** is the movement of money, goods and expertise from richer developed countries to the poorer developing countries, in order to assist those countries to make fuller use of their resources.

The poorer and weaker countries have not been able to raise much finance on commercial terms themselves, so assistance or aid from individual countries, and various organizations has had to be used as the principal source of funding.

Between 1945 and 1951, the United States pumped some $4 billion a year into Western Europe. The U.S.A. realized that Europe could not continue to buy American goods unless the war damaged European economy was rebuilt. The result was the Marshall Plan. In 1949, this aid amounted to 2% of the gross national product of the U.S.A. Such a commitment directed towards the developing world today could produce dramatic results. In the long term such aid is intended to stimulate trade and industry. Aid can also be given to relieve short term problems. Such emergency aid can be used to offset the effects of drought, flooding or any other hazard.

Television, in the mid 1980s, brought into the homes of people in the rich world a visual report on the human suffering of millions of people in the sub-Saharan region of Africa. The moral arguments for giving aid and assistance to less fortunate people stimulated the donation of vast sums of cash to organizations such as 'Band Aid' and 'Save The Children'.

The Brandt Report of 1980, 'North-South: A Programme for Survival', argued that the rich cannot prosper unless there is progress for the poor, and that economic recovery in the developed world was inextricably linked with development in the poor lands. Such countries not only supply the industrialized world with vital commodities, but also become customers for manufactured goods. This 'mutuality of interests' means that, although humanitarian and moral commitment to world development is important, the economic interdependence of the rich and poor is a powerful reason for the former to help the latter. The Northern developed nations need the Southern developing nations.

Types of aid

Western aid is organized along different lines. The basic distinction is between **bilateral aid**, which is given by one country to another country; **multi-lateral aid** which is funded by a number of nations, often through an international agency such as the World Bank; **voluntary aid** organizations such as Oxfam, and Christian Aid, which raise funds from individual people through charity collections.

Bilateral aid

This is aid from one government directly to another government. This is usually **'tied' aid** in the sense that the donor has a major role in the distribution of the aid. The receiving country would propose a plan for some development, and submit it to potential donors. The donor may then make conditions upon the aid. For example an increasing amount of aid is given only on the condition that the money is spent in the donor's country on goods and services. (Thereby being labelled, **'boomerang aid'**.) If West Germany were assisting Brazil to develop a nuclear power station, then the aid would be used to purchase the design and machinery from West Germany, and employ German specialists to construct the power plant. The United States accept that 93% of all aid for international development funds will be spent within the U.S.A. In West Germany, 80% of official bilateral aid comes back in payment for German goods and services.

Bilateral aid frequently has 'political strings' attached to it. The U.S.A. in 1985 gave $220 million to the Philippines. Undoubtedly this helps to maintain good political relations between the two countries, and ensures that the Americans keep their vital Pacific military bases on the islands. Within hours of President Marcos's flight from the Philippines, the American government promised the new ruling group, 'whatever help was needed for economic revival and national security.'

Multilateral aid

This type of aid comes from international agencies such as the World Bank, the United Nations Educational, Scientific and Cultural Organization (UNESCO), the International Monetary Fund (IMF), or the Food and Agricultural Organization (FAO). Such agencies, with the receiving countries, jointly finance projects. Although the receiving countries do have to have any proposed projects accepted by the helping agencies, normally this aid is not linked in any way to political pressure from the donor. The funds from the various agencies mainly come from the developed world in the form of contributions and loans. More than half the aid

given is only lent and has to be repaid with interest. Multilateral aid is now is moving away from investment in large costly industrial projects. It was once thought in the early 1970s that by improving the industrial base of a country by investment in iron and steel, cement factories and engineering, the benefits would reach down, and boost the whole country. In reality, the rural areas did not benefit, and such **project aid** supported a wealthy minority in selected urban areas. Project aid suited the donor countries and agencies, since the aid could be closely administered. However non-project aid is favoured by the receiving countries, and assistance can be chanelled into a total investment programme for the country. Fig. 7.1 shows the competing theories for applying development aid.

Voluntary aid and charities

Organizations such as Oxfam, Save The Children, and Christian Aid work, not from political or economic motivation, but for humanitarian reasons. Often the assistance given is fairly small, but often proves to be highly cost effective. The projects normally involve community participation and local direction.

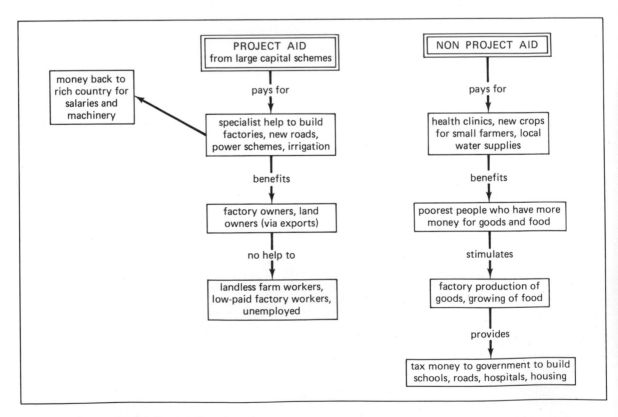

7.1 Development aid: competing theories

Who gives aid? Who receives aid?

The United Nations Development Programme in the 1970s, with the approval of member countries, agreed that developed countries should aim to give 0.7% of their Gross National Product (G.N.P.) to aid projects. Unfortunately, with a few exceptions, nations have not attained that level of support. Britain managed 0.33% in 1984, the U.S.A. 0.25% and Japan 0.32%. The most generous countries were Norway with 0.8%, Sweden at 0.86% and The Netherlands with 1.1%.

In recent years the oil rich Middle East countries have involved themselves in aid programmes. The O.P.E.C. nations have, with their increased oil revenues, contributed nearly 3% of their G.N.P., and the bulk of this aid is not tied. The Communist countries (mainly the U.S.S.R.) tend to give very low amounts in official development assistance, estimated to be in the order of 0.05% of their G.N.P. Following the publication of the Brandt Report in 1980, it was hoped that substantial increases in official aid would be announced, but as yet, there has been little change. (See Fig. 7.2.)

The distribution of aid does not always correspond to the areas of greatest need. The bulk of British and French aid goes to countries with links from the colonial era; aid from the United Arab Emirates and Qatar goes mainly to other Arab and Moslem countries; Australia and New Zealand favour adjacent Pacific countries such as Papua New Guinea. (See Fig. 7.3.)

The United Kingdom's contribution

The U.K.'s development policy is to concentrate on bilateral aid projects, and to assist the poorer countries of the world. The aid should be used to, 'promote long term social and economic development'. In 1984, a total of £1311 million was allocated for official development assistance, of which £780 million (i.e. 60%) was bilateral aid, and £531

	%
OECD countries (Organization for Economic Co-operation and Development: mainly rich western countries)	68.5
OPEC (Organization of Petroleum Exporting Countries: mainly oil rich Middle East countries)	20.6
Communist countries (mainly the USSR and other East European countries)	5.5
Non-government organizations (voluntary groups such as OXFAM)	5.4

7.2 Who gives?

	Aid per head U.S. $	% of G.N.P. derived from overseas aid
SURINAM	350.0	14
ISRAEL	290.0	9
PAPUA NEW GUINEA	120.0	17
JAMAICA	97.0	7
SOMALIA	82.0	30
SENEGAL	49	12
ZAMBIA	39	8
BURKINA FASO	33	24
NIGER	33	13

7.3 Who receives?

million multilateral. This sum was 0.33% of the British G.N.P. To add to this total, the charities raised a further £105 million.

73% of bilateral aid went to Commonwealth countries, principally India (£147 million), Kenya, Zambia, Tanzania and Sri Lanka. In total 124 countries received assistance from Britain: 46% went to Asia, 40% to Africa, and 14% to South America. The Government responded to 60 disaster appeals in 40 countries. A further £15 million was allocated to refugee relief work. The bulk of the aid to India went towards a thermal power plant at Bharat, linked to an aluminium smelter contract. The rest went mainly to coalmining, railway rolling stock and low cost housing. Nepal received assistance to plant trees in an effort to halt soil erosion, and Tanzania constructed and equipped a community hospital in Mbeya.

A total of £531 million was given in multilateral aid, 45% to the European Community Development fund, 40% to the World Bank, and almost 15% to United Nations Agencies.

Private investment by British companies in overseas subsidiaries accounts for another billion pounds. Often this investment is primarily to secure a profitable return and not necessarily to assist the receiving country.

Aid for Africa

Fig. 7.4 shows the sort of scene that dominated television and newspapers during the mid 1980s. The sub-Saharan famine belt of Ethiopia, Sudan, Chad, Niger, Burkina Faso and Mali, finally caught our imagination with horror. Such scenes had been common for years, and the major charities had attempted, in vain, to warn us all about the impending disaster. T.V. brought it home.

The causes are complex. For many years, the exploiting of the land, through overgrazing, over-

7.4 Mother mourning her children, victims of famine, at Korem, Ethiopia

cultivation, deforestation, and poor irrigation, resulted in soil erosion. At the root cause of this is a growing imbalance between human numbers, available resources, development and the environment. The long term result is falling food production and eventual desertification of the land.

Ethiopian appeals were launched by almost every international charity group. Oxfam spent over £20 million in 1984/85 on African aid. This included Land Rovers, high energy biscuits, plastic sheeting, wheat, milk powder and sugar.

What of the future? The needs for 1990 and onwards are different from those of 1985. Ethiopia and Sudan will still require over 2 million tonnes of food aid. The Food and Agricultural Organization called on donor countries to purchase food from areas of surplus in Africa, such as Kenya and Zimbabwe, and transport it to the areas of need. The additional requirements were for non-food items such as seeds, tools and agricultural equipment. Long term food aid programmes cannot solve the food crisis. The real cause is linked to poverty and soil erosion. The long term solution must involve tackling those problems.

1. a) What is meant by: bilateral aid; multilateral aid; aid from vountary organizations? Give an example of each.
    b) Comment on the advantages and possible disadvantages of each kind of aid.

2. Study Fig. 7.1. Comment on the advantages and disadvantages of: a) aid that 'trickles' down, and b) aid that builds up from the community.

3. Outline Britain's commitment to each of the three kinds of aid.

4. Why can long term food aid not solve a food crisis?

The United Nations

The U.N. celebrated its 40th anniversary in 1985, and is now an organization with 159 member states. Through the work of its Economic and Social Council 80% of the budget of the U.N. is now devoted to economic and social development in third world countries.

The range of the development work is enormous: education, food programmes, refugees, population censuses, health, child care, locust control, desertification programmes and disaster relief. Much of the U.N.'s work is caused by political, economic, social or environmental crisis.

Since 1945, the U.N. has disbursed over $U.S. 100 billion in development aid, allowing member states to set up the physical and human infrastructure that has permitted their economies to grow.

World trade

International trade is the most important factor linking nations. No country in the world has all the resources it needs within its own borders. Resources are unevenly distributed around the earth's surface, making trade essential to every country's economic system. Trading is also a major way of increasing national wealth.

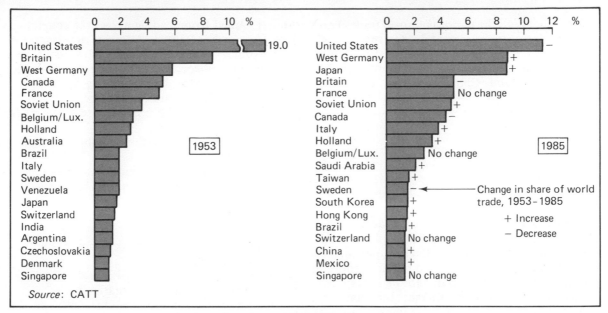

7.5 Major trading nations (% of total trade) – 1953–85

At present the developed world dominates trade. The developing world and to a certain extent the oil exporting countries have little control over the amount of goods sold abroad or the prices received. The developed world produces over 90% of the world's manufactured products, whilst the developing countries account for some two thirds of the world's trade in food and **primary mineral products**. Many developing countries rely on such exports for the bulk of their earnings.

The pattern of world trade changes little from one year to the next, but over decades the shifts have been significant. Fig. 7.5 shows the relative decline, as world trading nations, of the United States and Britain. By 1985, West Germany and Japan had increased their status.

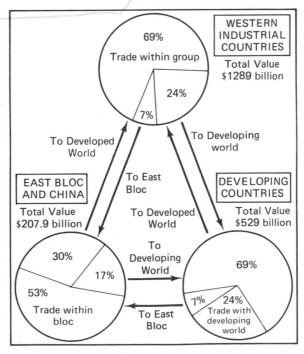

7.6 Pattern of world trade – 1985

Fig. 7.6 reveals the pattern of world trade. Three main trading groups are contained in this 'triangle of world trade': The Western Industrial States, who substantially trade amongst themselves, The Eastern Bloc and China, and the Developing Nations.

Britain's trade

Although small in area and accounting for only 1.2% of the world's population, Britain is the fifth largest trading nation in the world, and as a member of the E.E.C., part of the world's largest trading area. Britain remains a major supplier of machinery, vehicles, aerospace products, metal manufacture, electrical equipment and chemicals, and a significant oil exporter. It relies upon imports for over one third of total food requirements and for most raw materials needed for its industries.

From Fig. 7.7 it can be seen that more than three quarters of Britain's exports and imports are with developed countries. The trend in the last 30 years or so has indicated the growing importance of trade with other developed countries.

EXPORTS			IMPORTS	
1974	1985		1974	1985
33.8%	44.7%	E.E.C.	35.3%	45.5%
16%	12.3%	Other Western Europe	14.8%	17.0%
13.9%	16.3%	North America	13.6%	13.9%
10.5%	5.3%	Other developed countries	7.4%	6.8%
7.5%	8.2%	Oil exporting countries	15.6%	3.5%
18.3%	13.2%	Rest of World	13.2%	13.2%

7.7 Pattern of U.K. trade – 1974–85

Britain has nearly always earned a surplus in what has been called invisible trade. Such transactions fall into a number of categories: services such as sea transport, civil aviation; interest, profits and dividends from foreign investments by British firms; and general transfers of money into Britain.

Britain's trading balance has remained relatively strong in recent years due to the value of North Sea oil revenue. The price of oil on the world market dropped considerably in the mid 1980s, thereby reducing the value of the U.K. exports from about £11.5 billion in 1985 to about £6 billion in 1986.

Trading patterns in the developing world

From the viewpoint of the developing countries, trade with rich countries is vital, since their future development depends on their ability to trade.

Money earned from trading allows the country to pay for much of the technology necessary for future progress. At present, many of the industrial, agricultural and social developments are financed by borrowing from world banking agencies, or reliant upon bilateral aid or charities.

The characteristic features of third world trade are:
1. Overdependence on a small number of primary products.
2. Vulnerability to fluctuating commodity prices. Over the last 20 years such prices have generally risen at a rate far lower than manufactured goods. In a few cases prices have actually dropped.
3. Total value of trade from developing countries is generally small.
4. Reliance on the developed world for prices, transport, processing and marketing.

Fig. 7.8 shows some of the differences in the structure of trade for rich and poor countries, as based on employment. The pattern would appear to be that the developing countries trade particularly in exporting primary products, and importing manufactured goods, whilst the developed world imports primary products. The countries of the developed world also trade substantially amongst themselves in manufactured goods.

	Percentage of workforce employed in:		
	Primary industry	Secondary industry	Tertiary industry
TANZANIA	78	8	14
INDIA	71	12	17
INDONESIA	58	12	30
NIGERIA	52	19	29
BRAZIL	38	24	38
JAMAICA	26	19	55
U.S.S.R.	17	46	37
JAPAN	13	37	50
U.K.	2	40	58
U.S.A.	2	32	66

7.8 Employment structure

Most African economies depend for their foreign exchange on the export of just one or two raw materials, either cash crops or minerals. Sixty per cent of world sugar exports are sold by a handful of giant corporations, and over half of the world's supply is exported from Cuba, Brazil, Philippines, Dominican Republic and Thailand. Consumption in developed countries is static or falling partly because of slow population growth, but also because of taste and price changes which have favoured either artificial sweeteners or fewer sweeteners altogether.

Consumption in developing countries has been restrained by the slump and until recently by the strong dollar. During 1985 the price of sugar reached an all time low of 3 cents a pound, causing farmers to change products to other crops. The economic price is reckoned to be nearer 12 to 14 cents a pound.

There are a number of reasons why the developing countries have such a pattern of trade in primary commodities. One reason is the historical link between the former colonies and their 'mother' countries. 'The most useful function which colonies perform is to supply the mother country with a ready made market to get its industry going and maintain it, and to supply the inhabitants of the mother country with increased profits, wages and commodities.' This was stated by a French politician 100 years ago, and to a certain extent the system has perpetuated itself today.

The danger of depending on one or two primary products lies in the unpredictable behaviour of their prices. Fluctuations play havoc with planning and budgeting in developing countries. World prices for manufactured goods have increased steadily over the last 25 years, mainly due to increased production and labour costs. However the price of primary products in many cases has actually fallen. Zambia provides a cruel example of this. In 1977 the price of copper fell spectacularly. Since Zambia relies on copper for 90% of its foreign currency, the country ran into massive balance of payments deficits. Zambia could not repay her debts, and the Government was forced to cut back on development plans. Eventually the International Monetary Fund assisted Zambia, but only after imposing very stringent economy measures.

Oil prices have fluctuated greatly over the last 12 years. The massive increases in 1979 reverberated around the world, throwing the developed world into a deep recession. However oil prices have been falling steadily since 1981, and adjusting for inflation, prices by early 1986 were considerably below the 1973 prices. The obvious losers are the oil producers. Global demand for oil is now some 20% lower than it was in 1977, due to efficiencies in manufacturing and in motor vehicles, plus the increasing use of coal, nuclear power and gas for electricity generation. If oil prices do stabilise again, at about $20 a barrel, the reduction in the amount the industrial world would have to pay the exporters, would amount to some $60 billion worldwide. The countries most likely to suffer from such a loss of revenue are not necessarily the oil rich Middle East states, but more likely to be Indonesia, Venezuala, Nigeria and Mexico.

Primary products such as oil or rubber have to go through a number of processing stages before being marketed. At present the bulk of such processing and marketing is either controlled by, or takes place within, the developed world. When this happens, prices are less likely to fluctuate and greater profits can be gained. Only a few developing countries have succeeded in diversifying enough to make themselves less vulnerable to price fluctuations, such as Singapore, India, Morocco, Thailand and South Korea.

However, if countries are successful in widening the economic base from a reliance on limited primary exports towards a manufacturing and marketing base, then there are new hurdles to be overcome.

Fig. 7.9 summarises the contrasting patterns of trade in developed and developing countries.

Developing world	Developed world
* Often limited to one or two main items	* Very wide range of items
* Dominated by primary products	* Mainly manufactured goods
* Prices liable to fluctuate, often downwards	* Prices tend to be steady
* Demand for products can easily change due to technological advances elsewhere	* Demand tends to be steady, competition ensures efficiency
* Total trading value small	* Total trading value large
* Bulk of trade with developed world	* Bulk of trade within developed world
* Ownership of companies often foreign	* Profits retained by exporting countries, since most companies home owned
* Internal communications often inadequate	* Internal communication advanced

5. With reference to Fig. 7.6, describe the main features of world trade.

6. Using Fig. 7.7, describe the changing pattern of Britain's trade.

7. Using the text, plus Fig. 7.9, outline the main features of, and the problems associated with, international trade in the developing world.

7.9 Patterns of trade

Barriers to world trade

As the economic development of the third world progresses, there will be a contraction of employment in many traditional sections in the developed countries ('The North'), in order to accommodate the new industrial capacity of the developing 'South'. Since the 1960s a significant number of trade barriers have been imposed by the North. Quota limits, tariffs and import restrictions have been imposed on clothing and textiles, footwear, electronics and other products by certain countries spurred on by political pressure from businesses, trade unions, and political parties.

Britain maintains few restrictions on its international trade. Most goods (80%) may be imported freely, the main exception being some textile goods. Only a narrow range of goods are subject to any sort of export control. (Mainly military arms, some metals, and animals.)

So what are the implications for the 'North' of industrialization in the third world? There are three main fears:

1. Loss of markets as other countries produce their own goods. An example of this is Britain's decline as a shipbuilding nation, and the loss of overseas markets as countries such as Nigeria, Korea and Brazil build their own ships.
2. Cheaper imports from the lower paid developing countries reach the high labour cost developed world. Such 'flooding' of the market with cheap products can undermine the efficiency of the industry in the developed country. An obvious example of this is the textile and clothing industry in Britain. Cheap products from Korea, Hong Kong, the Philippines and other countries could be imported and sold in Britain at prices well below that considered economic for British produced goods.
3. An increase in unemployment as this competition intensifies.

In the long run, restrictions on world trade can only be detrimental to all concerned.

Multinationals

So far it has been shown that trading in the world today is controlled by the developed nations. Another significant feature of worldwide trade is the influence of **multinational** (or **transnational**) companies, characterized by being very extensive, wealthy and powerful. Companies such as Kodak, Volkswagon, Del Monte, Coca Cola, I.C.I., and B.P., employ many hundreds of thousands of workers worldwide, and invest millions of pounds in foreign countries in a wide variety of business

Advantages	Disadvantages
* Employment provided	* Key workers often not local
* Steady income	* Wage rates often low
* Investment in country will filter through economy	* Profits go overseas
* Improvement in technical skills	* May lead to migration within and from country
* Can encourage linked development in energy industries, and mineral exploitation	* Increased cost in imported energy
* Status, as industrial nation	* Multinationals may have too much political power.

7.10 Advantages and disadvantages of multinational companies to host country

activities. By far the largest investors in the third world are the multinational companies based in the U.S.A., followed by Japanese companies, West German and British. The country with the heaviest total of foreign investment is probably Brazil, where multinationals have a major impact on rubber, motor vehicles, manufacturing machinery, iron and steel, coffee, chemicals and mining. Giant companies such as Standard Oil of New Jersey have a trading value far greater than a majority of countries in the world. Such is their power through investment, land ownership, control of the world market, transport, packaging and marketing, that the interests of the host country can easily be overlooked. Fig. 7.10 summarises the advantages and disadvantages of multinationals in a developing country.

Not only do the multinationals dominate industrial global trade, but a trend detected in recent years is their growing involvement in farming. Some giant corporations such as Cadbury-Schweppes and Kellogs are actively involved in all production stages, from 'crop to shop'. This system of organization, whereby the same company produces the seeds, owns the land, grows the crop, processes the crop, transports it and finally markets the finished item, is called **agribusiness**.

The Brandt Report on North-South trade

The 1980 Report urged price stabilization of third world commodities (such as coffee, tea, rubber and sugar) at realistic, 'remunerative' levels. As we have seen above, the industrial world has a very firm grip on commodity processing and marketing, through the powerful multinational corporations. To allow free trade to flow between North and South, the Report wished that the developed world would loosen their grip on processing, and remove tariffs and other barriers to third world manufactured goods, as well as widen present trade concessions.

A world in debt

The President of the World Bank recently announced that the third world countries were paying more money back to the international banks in interest repayments than the banks were lending to them. Such a situation has arisen because developing countries which borrowed heavily to finance their development programmes are having to repay the loans at the same time as banks are reducing lending levels. This follows from the belief that such borrowers are a poor risk. The global scale of borrowing and debt repayments is staggering. Fig. 7.11 shows current debts in 1985/86, and the debt interest as a % of the value of annual exports of selected countries.

There are implications for both the lenders and the borrowers. Some British and European banks are very heavily committed to these loans, and any possibility of a default in payments could cause some banks to collapse. Brazil alone is in debt to British banks for some £9.3 billion.

Brazil attracted investers and lenders in the 1970s and early 1980s. The military regime could apparently guarantee high profit rates and investments in capital intensive industries provided lucrative markets for British and European machinery and equipment.

However a combination of events brought problems. The mid 1980s saw rising interest rates, falling commodity and oil prices, and falling investment. Third world countries have been faced with increasing trade deficits, and, with falling export markets and a stagnant and depressed internal market, there is little now to encourage foreign investment.

Effect in Latin America

Mexico was saved from bankruptcy in 1982 by the International Monetary Fund and by a series of austerity measures initiated by the new President. Although this resulted in high inflation (60% in 1985) low wages and a plummeting standard of living, the country was kept afloat by revenue from oil. This accounted for 70% of foreign income. During 1985 and early 1986 oil prices fell steadily, so that Mexico's income for oil (some $11 billion) will almost exactly equal the amount to be paid out in interest repayments. That debt now totals some $96 billion.

The governments of Mexico, Argentina, Venezuela, and Colombia, have indicated that the financial burden imposed on them is threatening their stability, and that without growth and a removal of trade limiting barriers, then the debt repayments cannot be met.

The earthquake which hit Mexico City in September 1985 caused over $3 billion damage, but possibly more damaging in the long term was the 20% loss in tourism income.

If the debts are to be met, then the resulting lower wages and rising unemployment places the burden of the debt on the already desperately poor. Brazil's president spoke for millions throughout Latin America when he asserted that, 'Brazilians will not pay the debt with their employment, their hunger or their democracy'.

Such forms of aid mentioned at the beginning of this Chapter often look appealing in the short term, but can pose immense problems. In a continent of shortage, scant resources are now flowing abroad in massive quantities, and the reduced capacity to import machinery and raw materials is severely holding back present and future economic growth.

8. What trade barriers are imposed by developed countries against the developing world?

9. Comment on the value to a developing country of having multinational companies active in that country.

10. Fig. 7.11 indicatates the extent of the financial problems of selected countries. How does such a situation arise, and, what problems can follow?

	Total debts 1985 in billion U.S. $	Debt interest as % of export value
ARGENTINA	48	52
CHILE	20	46
BRAZIL	102	41
MEXICO	96	60
PERU	13	31
PHILIPPINES	26	28
ECUADOR	22	24
VENEZUELA	35	36
YUGOSLAVIA	20	15
NIGERIA	19	33

7.11 Nations in debt

7.12 Pumping safe water from a newly installed tubewell, Bangladesh

11. This Chapter was called, 'Trade or Aid. The path to Development?' Which path would you follow?

Conclusion: trade or aid? Which path to development?

In this Chapter the competing claims of trade and aid have been investigated. As has been shown, global trade is considered vital to the mutual benefit of all nations. Unfortunately barriers restricting free trade have been identified, and the nature of the products exported from the developing countries often leaves those countries at the mercy of 'outside' agencies, which control production, processing, marketing and prices.

It has also been shown that aid is not without problems. Bilateral aid is often politically tied. Even loans from international agencies will have restrictions that limit their usefulness. Frequently the value of such aid seems to drain away. Even charitable aid can result in a mass of problems. Food aid doesn't only save lives, it becomes a way of life. Hundreds of thousands of Ethiopians spend their days in queues outside warehouses, waiting to be given food. As the years pass it is increasingly difficult for them to return to their fields, even if the rains come.

The relief agencies do give seed and sometimes tools, but Ethiopian farming is dependent on oxploughing, and there are few projects to restock communities with animals. If food aid makes up for the shortfalls in production, it is a disincentive to produce.

Increasingly aware of these drawbacks, the various U.N. relief agencies are increasingly investing in public works programmes where people are paid in cash instead of food. They use the cash to buy food, clothes, seed, and other necessities in nearby towns. Instead of creating dependency on imported food, the project is stimulating the local economy and helping the people regain their economic base for starting to produce again when the rains come. Handing out food is not the only way of helping people cope.

The Brandt Report suggested that there is a moral responsibility to solve the problems of the poor countries, and remove the injustices that have held back development, by worldwide co-operation. It recommended that all developed nations should meet the target of giving 0.7% of their gross national product as official development assistance and that the quality of this aid should be improved so that more is untied and available to the poorest countries. To deal with global trade, a new organization, which might be called the World Development Fund, should be set up. This would co-ordinate the financing of the development programme and would provide the opportunity for all countries to co-operate on a more equitable basis. As yet there has been limited action in this direction.

8
Conclusion: Global Village 2000

What does development mean?

Traditionally, development and industrialization were considered to go hand in hand. To the South, the developed North had a high standard of living and economic stability. Since the North relied heavily upon an industrial base for this wealth, it was naturally assumed by both the North and the South that the path towards development was one based on such an industrial foundation. It was believed that through industry the whole economy would be regenerated and that this would result in improvements and efficiences in agriculture and that higher standards in social conditions would inevitably follow.

According to the Brandt Commission, development is not simply about machines, manufacturing growth or copying highly industrialized nations. The prime objective for a country should be to use its human potential to the full. Quality of growth should not be sacrificed. The Food and Agricultural Organization suggest that development should not be seen to be equated with economic growth. Such growth, the F.A.O. state, is an integral part of development, but in fact merely one link in a fairly long chain.

The indicators of development outlined in Chapter 1 can be divided up into at least two main categories: those emphasising industrial and

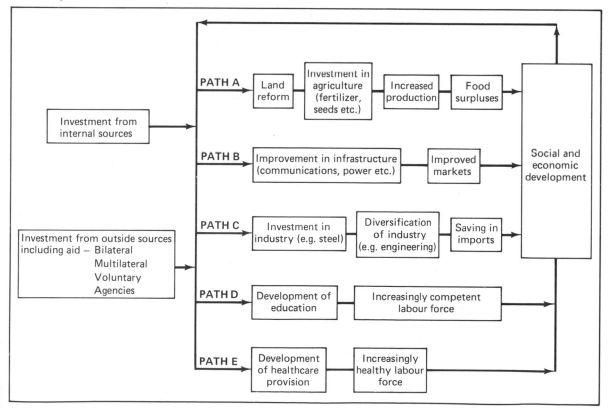

8.1 Model of economic development

economic features, and those that concentrate on social and human features. The F.A.O. believe that development should be considered from the standpoint of human beings and their needs. The level of satisfaction of these needs is a measure of development. In concrete terms, these needs are food, clothing, living space, health care and water supply. Policies that tend to reduce poverty, increase employment and reduce inequality on national and international levels have always been at the centre of the United Nations concern. This new definition of development completely reverses the old one that considered industrial manufacturing to be an end in itself. It puts first those who will potentially reap its advantages, that is the less privileged social classes.

A model for economic and social development

Which path?

Fig. 8.1 illustrates the possible paths for economic and social development. Whichever route is chosen, a prerequisite must be a source of finance. As has been explained in Chapter 7, the developing nations must look towards the developed world for the bulk of the initial investment. Tackling large-scale problems involves a process whereby each solution appears to bring with it a new series of problems. This seemingly endless and frustrating process must be seen not as a sign of failure, but as a real measure of progress towards a better, if not a more complex, world.

Investment can often involve political ties and 'economic colonialism', and an increasing debt repayment problem. Path A, leading to agricultural investment and increased production, has been shown in Chapter 3 to be a potentially sound route to follow. Paths D and E have similarly been investigated in Chapters 2 and 4, and the link with social and economic development established. Traditionally paths B and C were seen to be the main routeways to be followed to achieve economic maturity. There are undoubtedly benefits which can accrue from industrialization.

Benefits following industrialization

By diversifying the economy and relying less on agriculture and primary products, the economy of a nation is less likely to be subject to changing demand patterns and reliant on unpredictable weather. Industrialization can increase the value of exports and can also reduce the import bill for manufactured goods. Industrialization can also provide the impetus for developments in other sectors of the economy, for example energy and communications. Since agricultural products can be manufactured (fertilizers, farm machinery), there should be increases in agricultural output. By manufacturing, a country can break into the trading path to development.

However industrialization has its problems. A developing country will need to seek outside help for aid and investment, and the lack of suitably skilled workers will mean a reliance on imported technology. Any third world country starting on the path to industrial development will have to break into the existing world market. The local inhabitants may have insufficient funds to buy the manufactured products, and valuable foreign currency will be spent on increased imports. The effect of increased industrialization may also bring about mass migration from rural districts, and the resulting mechanisation of traditional jobs will result in increased unemployment. The new industries are often controlled and owned by foreign multinationals.

The answer to the question, 'which path?', is therefore not so simple. Clearly what is required by each country is a statement of attainable aims, and a plan for achievement. Such large-scale planning calls for a stable government, capable of turning long term plans into a firm course of action.

As was indicated in Chapter 7, an important factor in development must be to boost rural income. The key is seen to lie in technologies able to utilise local skills and resources, and with minimal dependence on imported resources. Technology by itself is no longer seen as the automatic problem solver. More than ever before, emphasis is being placed on **appropriate** or **intermediate technology**, with simple rugged village hand pumps having as much collective impact as the hydroelectric dam project at a fraction of the cost.

Today development projects are more **decentralized**, focusing on smaller programmes rather than large scale, highly technical, capital-intensive projects. Development experts have a more profound understanding of the complex development process, of the interdependence of social, economic and political factors which have to be considered in its entirety.

Development is measured in decades, not years. The delays make people impatient, the mistakes are frustrating and disappointing. Development work needs to be co-ordinated. Disease and malnutrition, for example, are now seen as symptoms of the much more pervasive problem of poverty and

8.2 Ploughing and harrowing, the Punjab

underdevelopment rather than problems in isolation. Increasing inadequate food production in Guatemala may require an immunization programme to protect villagers from malaria, technical advice to determine affordable tools, and educational programmes that enable people to take advantage of available technology and make informed decisions as to the available approaches for improving their crops. Development is complex and requires co-ordination on many levels, thus the great risk of failure.

So which path to development? You decide.

> 'No man is an Island, entire of it self; every man is a piece of the Continent, a part of the main . . . any man's death diminishes me, because I am involved in Mankind; And therefore never send to know for whom the bell tolls; It tolls for thee'.
> JOHN DONNE (1572–1631)

1. Study Fig. 8.1. Take each of the five paths in turn and outline a) the advantage of following that route and b) the obstacles that have to be overcome.

2. Using the information in this Chapter, and drawing upon the knowledge you have picked up in the book, define in your own terms the following concepts: developed; developing.

Glossary

AGE SPECIFIC (BIRTH AND DEATH) RATES	an index of fertility or mortality showing the number of births or deaths in specific age bands, over the number of people in those same age bands
AGRIBUSINESS	very large organisations involved in the various stages of growing food
AID	the movement of money, goods and expertise, usually from the rich world to the poor
APPROPRIATE TECHNOLOGY	the use of suitable machines and equipment. Advanced equipment is not always the most appropriate equipment in a third world country
ASYLUM	a country offering shelter and support to refugees
BACTERIA	minute uni-cellular living organisms, commonly found in the human body. They can occasionally be harmful and produce poisonous toxins which can damage vital body organs
BAREFOOT DOCTOR	a medical aide providing local community medicine in rural areas, especially in S.E. Asia
BILATERAL AID	the movement of money, goods and expertise from one country to another country
BOAT PEOPLE	S.E. Asian refugees who flee their country (especially Vietnam) by sea
'BOOMERANG' AID	aid given on the condition that the money is spent in the donor's country in the form of goods and services
BRAIN DRAIN	the loss of highly qualified workers from an area through migration
BUFFER ZONE	a designated countryside area with strict planning controls to ensure that urban areas do not meet
C.A.P.	Common Agricultural Policy of the E.E.C.
CALORIE INTAKE	measure which expresses the energy value of foods
CENSUS	the total process of collecting economic and social data; a population count
CEREALS	grasses grown for edible grain
CIRCULATION	the short-term or long-term movement of a person involving a return to their place of origin
COMMUTER	a person who travels daily to and from work (usually in a city)
COUNTERURBANISATION	the loss of people from urban to rural areas
CRUDE BIRTH RATE	a basic calculation indicating the number of live births in a population, per 1000 of that population, in one year
CRUDE DEATH RATE	a basic calculation indicating the number of deaths in a population, per 1000 of that population, in one year
DECENTRALISATION	the relocation of development planned to avoid congestion
DEMOGRAPHIC TRANSITION MODEL	a model which shows the 4 stages of population change
DEMOGRAPHY	the study of population statistics, normally covering birth, death and population change
DEPENDENCY RATIO	a ratio to illustrate the relationship between the non-economically active population and the economically active population
DEPENDENT POPULATION	normally those members of the population too young to work and above retirement age
DIET DEFICIENCY DISEASE	a disease resulting from an imbalanced diet
DIFFUSION	the geographical spread, or progress, of a disease across an area
DIVERSIFICATION	the introduction of new, varied industries
DOUBLING TIME	the number of years it will take a population to double in size

ECONOMIC INDICATOR	a measurement which points out economic well-being in a country
ECONOMICALLY ACTIVE POPULATION	generally taken to be that group of the population between 15 and the retirement age
EMIGRANT	one who leaves their own country to settle in a foreign country
ENDEMIC	(of a disease) habitually present in an area due to a permanent local cause
ENDOGENOUS	(of a disease) not infectious and normally associated with a certain lifestyle
EPIDEMIC	(of a disease) prevalent among a community at a special time and produced by some causes not generally present in the area
EXECUTIVE	(of a disease) associated with the modern lifestyle found in the industrialised, urbanised world
EXOGENOUS	(of a disease) infectious
FERTILITY	a measure of the tendency for a population to change due to births
FOOD WASTAGE	loss of food through inefficient farming, accident, theft and decay
FOOTLOOSE INDUSTRY	an industry with few or no ties to limit its location to a specific place
GENERAL FERTILITY RATE	an index of fertility. Normally the total number of births in a year, divided by the total number of women aged 15 to 44
GHETTO	section of a city inhabited mainly by members of racial or religious minority groups and characterised by poverty and social deprivation
GREEN REVOLUTION	the introduction of new, high yielding varieties seeds and new farming techniques aimed at increasing food production
GROSS NATIONAL PRODUCT (G.N.P.)	the value of production of goods and services per head of population in a country
GROWTH RATES	the rate at which a population is increasing, normally calculated by subtracting the death rate from the birth rate
GUESTWORKER	an immigrant worker offered employment in another country, usually to fill a menial, low paid job
H.Y.V. SEEDS	seeds developed scientifically to produce large yields
HORTICULTURE	the growing of flowers, fruit and vegetables, usually in market gardens and orchards
HOST	a plant, animal or human in which a parasitic flea, tick or worm can live, apparently without any ill effects
HUNGER	lack of food
HYDROPONICS	the growing of plants without soil but in a water/sand/nutrient mix
ILLITERACY	the inability to read and write
IMMIGRANT	one who enters a foreign country to settle
INFANT MORTALITY RATES	the number of infant deaths within the first year of life, per 1000 of the total number of live births
INFECTIOUS	(of a disease) capable of being passed from one person to another by a disease-carrying organism
INFORMAL SECTOR	low paid, insecure, semi-legal employment
INFRASTRUCTURE	a network of public services such as roads, sewerage, water and power
INTERMEDIATE TECHNOLOGY	the use of appropriate machines and equipment in a third world country. Advanced machinery may not always be practical
INTRANATIONAL MIGRATION	the movement of people within the boundary of a single country
JET-BORNE	(of a disease) transmitted rapidly around the world, usually by humans, using modern transport
LIFE EXPECTANCY	the average number of years, from birth, that a population or an individual would expect to live
MALNUTRITION	deficiency in diet due to inadequate food or insufficient vitamins
MEGALOPOLIS	a continuous stretch of urban development formed by the sprawl of cities and their conurbations
METROPOLITAN AREA	a large city area and its hinterland
MIGRATION	a planned or forced movement of population
MILLIONAIRE CITY	a city with a population of at least one million
MULTILATERAL AID	the movement of money, goods and expertise from one set of countries to an agency which then redistributes these to other countries
MULTINATIONAL COMPANIES	very large companies based in many countries around the world
MULTIPLE CROPPING	the planting of successive crops in the same area in any one year

NEW COMMONWEALTH	an association of independent black nations which used to belong to the British Empire
NON-ECONOMICALLY ACTIVE POPULATION	generally taken to be those too young to work (below 15) and those who have reached retirement age
NORTH–SOUTH	the approximate division of the world into rich (North) and poor (South) countries
OBESITY	excess body fat which usually results from over-eating of carbohydrate foods
OVERNUTRITION	consumption of food in excess of that required for a healthy, balanced diet
OVERSPILL	excess population who move after the redevelopment of a city (usually inner city) area
PANDEMIC	(of an epidemic disease) spreading across a vast geographical area
PARASITE	an animal or plant that lives in or on another organism
PERIPHERAL SLUM	shanty town located at the edge of a city
PHYSICAL QUALITY OF LIFE INDEX (P.Q.L.I.)	a measurement showing results of service provision based on life expectancy, infant mortality rate and adult literacy rate
PLANTATION	a large estate given over to the growing of a single crop such as coffee, tea, rubber
PRIMARY MINERAL PRODUCTS	unprocessed raw materials such as copper
PRIMATE CITY	a single settlement of outstanding size and importance in a country
PROJECT AID	money, goods or services given to a country to be used in a particular project, approved by the donor
PROTOZOA	minute single-cell organisms that can attack the blood supply by damaging the red cells
REFUGEE	a person who escapes to a foreign country from religious or political persecution
REPATRIATION	the return of immigrants to their native land
RETURN MIGRATION	the return of immigrants to their native land, usually following an economic recession
'SELF-HELP' SCHEME	a project aimed at improving an area carried out by the inhabitants of that area
SHANTY TOWN	an area of very poor quality housing, sometimes temporary and illegal, with low service provision
SHARECROPPER	a tenant farmer who pays part of their crop as rent to a landlord
SMOG	a mixture of smoke and fog causing air pollution in industrial and urban areas
SOCIAL INDICATOR	a measurement which points out social well-being in a country
STARVATION	lack of food
SUBURBANIZATION	the gradual spread of an urban area into a surrounding rural area
SUPER CITY	a city with a population of at least five million
THIRD WORLD	a term usually applied to the socially and economically less developed countries of Asia, Africa and Latin America
'TIED' AID	aid from a richer country to a poorer country for a particular project, and for which the donor county has a major role in the allocation of the funds
TRANSNATIONAL	a large company operating in several countries
TUBEWELL	a hollow, pointed pipe with perforations used to extract underground water
UNDERNUTRITION	lack of food
URBANIZATION	the change from a rural to an urban character together with its causes and effects
VECTOR	any living carrier (an insect, animal or human) of an infectious disease
VIRUSES	extremely small particles, which can exist inside body cells. Once inside, they can inflict extensive damage very rapidly
VOLUNTARY AID	the movement of goods, money and expertise from charity collections to the poorer lands of the world
WATER BORNE	(of a disease) closely related to water. This may be due to the role of water in spreading the disease, or providing a habitat for the disease-carrying organism
WHITE REVOLUTION	the development of dairy farming schemes in India aimed at improving quality of diet